Sauternes

BERNARD GINESTET'S GUIDE
TO THE VINEYARDS OF FRANCE

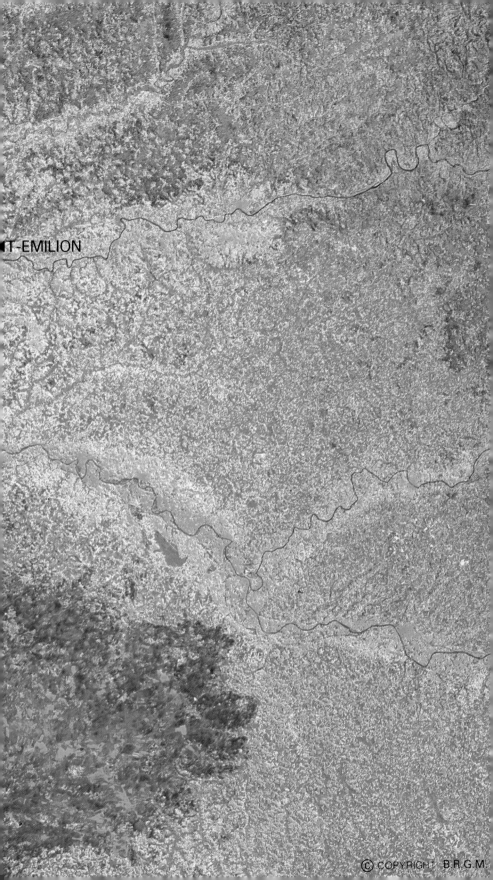

T-EMILION

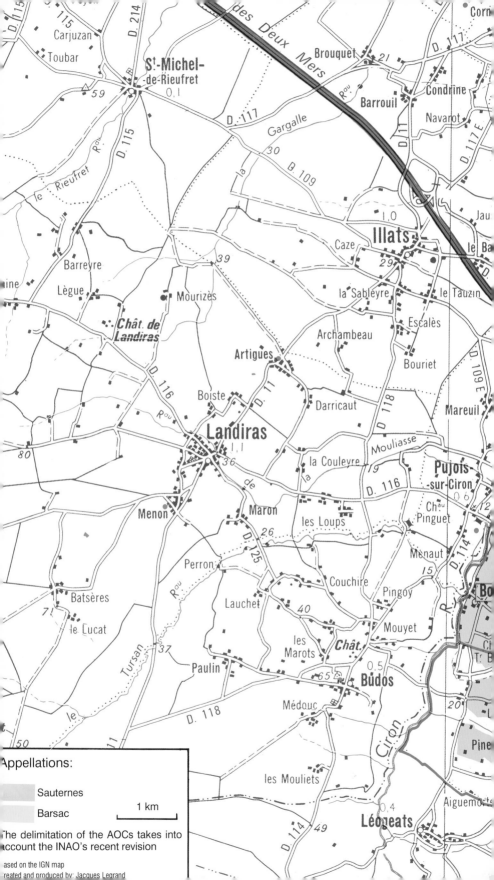

Cadillac
CT 3,8
Lamothe
Berthoumieu
Jean-Fauxde-Momp
Comm.-de-Momp
Génis
d'Armagnac
116
Jeanne de Mornes
eyre
N 113
0.9
Louriac
14
Naudin
Balan
D. 117
Pitchat
le Goutey
Lamothe
la Grave
la Bouade
2.3
0.3
12
Barsac
Gabarnac
Sem
13
D. 117
la Croix
le Fourneau
0
D. 120
Gros pine
Pavillon
D. 10
117
Crabitan
103
Peyno
les Guionne
Hallet
Larrivat
Baure
D. 117
Simon
le Peyrat
T. Orient.
Labat
Meyroux
Gravas
Rolland
Grottes
Mounet
Tombeau de
Ro
la inesse
Ch Védrines
2.2
Ste Croix
-du-Mont
0.9
Verdelais
Bel
Preignac
0.7
Liloy 96
Jean du Bosc
62
le Puch
île de Gruère
St-Maixant
1.2
Médudon
Côte de
Galhem de Rey
Dutoya
Labor
Lamothe
109 E
Jean Cabos
les Noyers
le Piquey
1.9
Bastor
Lamontagne
Toulenne
1.3
LANG
D 8 E
Ch Suduiraut
D. 116
Touilla
Arrançon
D 125 E
Mounic
Château Yquem
la Tuilerie
Galay
D. 8
75
Ch Rieussec
41
le Pajot
D. 8
les Sables
le Tei
uternes
0.9
Fargues
les Garres
34
les Claveries
76
Fontaine
Camagnon
Mouta
Moura
D. 125
Roudey
Hontarouge
D. 125 E
Brion
Brouquet
le Laurier
Mounic
Mal
Cazaus
Coutchoune
81
Guey
Ch
89
D. 223 E
Rabaud Boutoc
Ch

Bernard Ginestet

Foreword by Nicholas Faith

Sauternes

Translated by John Meredith

BERNARD GINESTET'S GUIDE
TO THE VINEYARDS OF FRANCE

Jacques Legrand

Originated and produced by:

Jacques Legrand SA

English version edited by:

Editor:	Nicholas Faith
Assistant editor:	Tamara Thorgevsky
Translator:	John L. Meredith
Copy editor:	Barbara Mellor
Editorial secretary:	Christine Fourton

Art director:	Henri Marganne
Layout:	Claire Forgeot

ⓒ 1990 Jacques Legrand SA, Paris
for the French edition
ⓒ 1990 Jacques Legrand SA
for the English edition
Distributed in UK by Longman
Distributed in Canada by Raincoast Books

ISBN 0-582-07544-0 for Longman UK distribution
ISBN 2-905969-39-3 for the rest of the world

Printed in Belgium by Brepols, Turnhout

Foreword

On the face of it, it is a bit of a cheek for Bernard Ginestet to describe himself as 'a failed peasant of sorts, but close to the earth with all my roots deep within it'. But I for one believe him, despite his origin as son and grandson of two of Bordeaux's most distinguished wine merchants and château-owners, because his love of the soil shines through every word of this book.

Perhaps his most important contribution - apart from the thoroughness of his examination of the region's wines, cru by cru - is his final demolition of the usual notions of the origins of noble rot. By bringing to bear all his considerable armoury of historical knowledge, Bernard makes a (to me incontrovertible) case that the wines, as he puts it, were 'saprian', their qualities traceable to the Romans who so appreciated the gamier, sweeter things of life.

This volume is particularly rich in descriptions of the history of dozens of individual châteaux, and the past and present qualities of their wines. But, Bernard being Bernard, he doesn't necessarily confine himself to the château under discussion. If you want an account of the history of the barrique bordelaise, you have to turn to the entry on Château Caillou. A brilliant, if controversial (you cannot, thank God, stop Bernard being Bernard, especially when, as so often, he has a point) analysis of the whole concept of the cru classé as it applies to this region can be found in the entry on Château Grillon.

Unfortunately, the French edition went to press before Bernard could discuss the biggest single revolution in the history of the great sweet wines of the banks of the Ciron: the way in which the technique of cryo-extraction has swept the vineyard, even such venerable traditionalists as Château d'Yquem, in the past few years.

The technique – simply freezing the grapes after they are picked – is a simple, natural, chemical-free, ecological method of separating the grapes most suitable for making fine sweet wines from their lesser brethren. It will enable the Sauternais to save some of their crop in years (like 1984) when fine, well-rotted grapes were buried in the heart of individual bunches, unharvestable because the outside grapes had been attacked by ignobler forms of rot.

'La Cryo', as it was inevitably dubbed, also enables the Sauternais to harvest grapes immediately afer the heaviest of rains, knowing that freezing the bunches will separate the raindrops from the grapes beneath. In future the Sauternais will still require the same discipline and endure the same nail-biting wait every autumn long after their fellow-growers in the rest of France are celebrating their harvests brought safely home. But at least they can now be confident that they will be able to capture the magic nectar trapped in the well-rotted grapes and not have to sit around waiting for the sun to shine, or lamenting the sweetness lost in the heart of otherwise grey (or green) bunches.

Nicolas Faith

"To make good wine,
harvest last."
Virgil, Eclogues

Contents

The wines of Sauternes and Barsac are "saprian" wines

All the legends claiming to explain how and why "noble rot" came about are mythical monsters, nineteenth-century style, which are simply and solely admissions of ignorance. Frankly, this book is too serious for me to relate them. Indeed, I am astonished that they have been heeded and retold by authors of repute, including distinguished university scholars. No, the famous rot called *Botrytis cinerea* is not a spontaneous phenomenon dating back to the pre-industrial era, and the discovery of its effects on the sémillon grape owes nothing to the marquis of Romain-Bertrand de Lur Saluces who, when he came back to Yquem in 1847, in late autumn after a hunting party in Russia, found estate manager and harvesters awaiting him, scissors in hand, to order the start the harvest. Moreover, this story is far too prosaic to be a legend. And I give no greater credence to those who declare, without any proof whatsoever, that one day the growers of Sauternes, inspired one day by the philosophers of the Enlightenment, turned the practices of Germany or Hungary to their advantage. In reality, to come close to the truth, we have to search further back in time.

So, then, we need to go back to the origins of the French language, to its earliest Graeco-Latin roots. For it is not enough to say that the wines of Sauternes and Barsac are "saprian"; we have to give some explanation. Richard Olney cast an eye over the question in his book on Yquem as if, in passing, he had lifted a corner of the veil covering a weathered antique stone tablet. His gaze could doubtless have lingered longer on it. But Richard Olney's purpose was to talk about Yquem, its history, its pomp and its glory; not to trace the

---

◄ *In the vineyards of Sauternes, burnished by autumn, the picking of the "noble grapes" is almost a religion.*

original source of sweet wines. Barsac and Sauternes are at the heart of our subject, on the other hand, and, as they may be said to be the best sweet wines in the world, I do not feel that I can pass over the story of the origin of their birth in silence. So we must retrace the course of the golden river which, over the centuries, has inspired so many poets all over the world. We shall go back to the Flood. According to tradition there is no flood without Noah. The story is well known. I will not go so far as to say that Mount Ararat was in Sauternes and that Château d'Arche (the ark) is the obvious proof of this. But I would like to point out that, for the Greeks, Noah, re-christened Oeneus, was intimately linked with Dionysius, the god of wine, inebriation and procreation. These things sometimes become confused. According to Greek mythology, Dionysius gave the first vine to be planted to Oeneus, the King of Calydon. This vine was to provide oenology with its roots, both literally and metaphorically, for the word itself derives from Oeneus. The ancient world, both Greek and Roman, had a wide vocabulary for describing wine. This is not the moment to draw up a list, but simply to single out two words: the noun *saprias* and the adjective *sapros*. The first meant "old wine", or more precisely, "nectar with a perfume of flowers". When used by writers, it had the connotation of a rare, much sought-after drink, a luxury wine. The second had two meanings. The first meant mould, decay, rot, etc., and the other, when applied to wine, took on the very precise meaning of ripe, old, mature. The Romans then developed the root *sapor*, meaning anything which related to flavour, taste and sometimes perfume. The English "sapid" is a derivative of it. Today, the adjective "saprian" can no longer be found in the dictionary. However, it is precise and cannot really be replaced. I found it recently in *Le Savouron*, a work of humorous erudition by Monsieur Modeste Savouron, who gives its definition as follows: "Relating to certain products made from noble rot (e.g. Sauternes wines, Yquem)". This is a modest summary which I consider to be nicely explicit.

"To make good wine, harvest last", wrote Virgil in his *Eclogues*. The line is used as an epigraph at the beginning of this book, for it is ideally applicable to the wines of Barsac and Sauternes. In antiquity, harvesting was done late. It did not begin before the month of October, since the objective was better wines which would age well. As today, this was to the detriment of quantity but to the benefit of quality. *Saprias oinos* was the expression which defined these products (a kind of antithesis of "Beaujolais nouveau"). The grapes remained on the vines until they were cooked by the sun. Sometimes they were picked and then spread out on wicker trays to allow their juice to become more concentrated. This desiccation is called in French "passerillage". If it is pushed to its limits, it produces dry, raisin-like grapes. In reality, the strict distinction between a grape which has been allowed to dry out and a grape affected by rot is not always easy to make. The two phenomena can coexist perfectly well, and their effects combine: all the more so in that the autumn climate plays a role of prime importance in determining the pre-eminence of the one over the other. In the Mediterranean basin desiccation is more common; but certain climatic conditions, peculiar to a handful of geographical situations, can favour the grape's concentration by rot equally well, if not more so. In both cases, the best quality comes with over-ripeness. The Greek philosophers and philologists of old must have been struck by the discovery that rotten grapes could produce a nectar of the gods, so they conferred dignity on the pejorative word *sapros* rather than searching for a superlative. We could develop its interpretation, conferring on it a tortured mysticism, much to the liking of the distant ancestors of our culture (with maturity comes death's obscurity). Without insisting any further, let us simply agree that the shrinking of the grapes was followed by an improvement in the wine. We also know that the gastronomes of the period liked food which was "gamey". More words from the same root: *saperdes*, for the Greeks, was fish marinated in brine and for the Romans *saprus caseus* was a highly fermented cheese. Our liking for meat and particularly game which has been hung is a legacy of these refined tastes, just as we enjoy the wines of Sauternes and Barsac which are "saprian" wines, too.

There is also a wine called "Saprian". It comes from Arvisia, a promontory on the island of Chios where vines have grown since remotest antiquity. Of course it is a sweet wine, the result of late harvesting. Chios (or Khios, Chio, and so on) is one of the oldest, most famous *crus* in the world. Arvisia and Mount Phanea (traces of Noah again) are its most prestigious terrains. Close to the main island are five smaller islands which in former days were known as the *Oenousses* (literally, full of vineyards). The wines of the archipelago were so famous that the growers of Chios had a special shape of amphora made which was depicted on the coins minted there. This was

---

At Château d'Yquem the golden light which bathes the vineyards at harvest time shines on into the night with the illumination of the old walls. Because of its high position, Yquem can be seen glowing from far off. ▶

doubtless one of the very first examples of an *appellation d'origine contrôlée*. The Cypriots, among others, lost no time in counterfeiting these wines. It was probably at Chios that the idea of *eugeneia* was born, equivalent to "noble vine" or vineyard. The wine of Chios was "saprian" and distinguished, and could be kept for at least three years.

This carefully aged, unctuous nectar was the delight of the wealthiest classes. By virtue of its rarity and the distinction it stood for, it came to represent affluence and luxury for those who had it in their cellars. No one could better honour their gods and guests than

by pouring this glorious liquid into their goblets. After having a ritual pyre erected for Patroclus's funeral, Achilles sacrificed "an infinite number of bulls and sheep", his (Patroclus's) finest hounds and his best horses before slitting the throats of "twelve of the most valiant young captives of the noblest Trojan families". And it was only after such rich and rare tributes that the wine was poured on to the brazier from a golden urn held by four friends. The Marquis Bertrand de Lur Saluces, the previous owner of Yquem, used to enjoy telling this story, related by Homer in the *Iliad*. The wine did not come from Château Yquem, but rather from Chios, near the gulf of

Smyrna. The fame of sweet wines was then only in its infancy. The Romans, the most ruthless of warriors at the beginning of their history, were nevertheless captivated by the idea of extreme sweetness. The austere Cato, who called for the destruction of Carthage, also proclaimed that to make good wine the grapes should be gathered ripe, or even shrivelled. This recommendation turned into a precept and the best *crus* of the empire followed the fashion for late harvesting. The grandchildren of Romulus and Remus were nurtured on the noble rot: we even know that the six hundred and twenty-second year after the founding of Rome – that is 131BC – was a fantastic vintage! Meanwhile, the term *sapor* was seized on by intellectuals and given abstract connotations. Cicero, in his speech "On His Return to the Senate", used the term "*homo sine sapore*" to describe an imbecile. Eminent Romans always accompanied their hors-d'œuvres (*promulsis*) with sweet wines, which they also served with dessert. And what were these hors-d'œuvres? Mussels in a sauce, woodpigeon, larks, fowl with asparagus, sea-urchins and oysters. These dishes – historically entirely authentic – are mentioned in order to extend the culinary knowledge of those who like Sauternes, but who do not know "how" to drink it. Moreover, I can vouch for the excellence of Sauternes with asparagus, a totally unexpected marriage, but a subtle one. As for oysters, we only need to read what Bertall wrote in 1878: "How many times in the Maison-Dorée, or the Café-Riche or the Café-Anglais, in the company of a good friend, I have been delighted by drinking Sauternes with the greenish oysters of Marennes! What an exquisite marriage."

Thus, excessive maturity of the grapes through desiccation and/or rot has been embraced since the time when wine was first made. As a viticultural practice it spread all over Europe as vineyards were created and was encouraged everywhere where climatic conditions permitted. When did it appear in the Bordeaux region? To date this with any certainty is, of course, impossible. All the same, the theory according to which the exploitation of noble rot and harvesting by staggered selective pickings became general practice in about the middle of the nineteenth century can clearly not be credited. As far as we know, the oldest known reference to late harvesting appears to be an act for *métayage* (a form of leasing whereby rent was paid in wine) drawn up by the notary of Barsac on October 4, 1666, for François Sauvage, squire of Yquem. In it, it is specified that "in order not to harm the reputation of the said wine, harvesting shall be done only when the grapes are fully ripe. It is the practice in Bommes and Sauternes to harvest every year about October 15." We know that at this time, harvesting used to begin nearly everywhere else about September 15 or 20, about a month earlier. We do not have sufficient documentation to monitor the harvesting calendar in the Sauternes region, but it seems that two schools existed side by side. Disagreements arose between the proprietors and the people who worked on the *métayage* system, the latter fearing that the grapes would be ruined, the former speculating about the weather (present and future), hoping for the sweetest wines. Here a distinction should be made between late harvesting and staggered selective pickings. The first simply implies waiting for a certain level of over-ripeness throughout the vineyard; the second implies several pickings in the vineyard to gather only the grapes attacked by rot. We find traces of this latter practice described quite explicitly in a report by the steward of Guienne, Lamoignon de Courson, dated 1716: "At harvest time the grapes are selected and only those which are almost rotten are gathered, with the result that harvesting can sometimes last right through to the month of December." Nothing could be more precise. It should also be mentioned that Lamoignon de Courson describes this as an established practice and not as a new technique. Other evidence suggests that the practice was already long established.

At this time and even in the preceding century, tenants of vineyards in Sauternes, Preignac, Barsac and Cérons were anxious to protect the authenticity of their wines. They forbade the introduction of "foreign" wines and took stringent measures to control the boatmen transporting casks of wine. Wines coming from Bazas were particularly subject to rigorous inspection.

Henri Redeuilh has recorded for us the results of various historical researches undertaken on the other side of the river in the regions of Cadillac, Loupiac and Sainte-Croix-du-Mont. It appears from these that at the beginning of the eighteenth century, the white grapes were harvested after the red and the harvest was gathered in several stages, often finishing about mid-November. For Dr Martin, a local scholar from the beginning of the century, there was no possible doubt: "We can declare with certainty that harvesting sweet white wine in the Bordeaux region goes back to the middle of the seventeenth century, and that the first vines to be picked in this way were those of Bommes and Sauternes, in particular those owned by Monsieur Sauvage, the proprietor of Diquem*." Among the most reliable witnesses is Bidet's *Traité sur la nature et sur la culture de la vigne*, the second edition of which, dated 1759, is in my posses-

---

* *Yquem was often spelt in this way in the seventeenth and eighteenth centuries.* 19

sion. In a few paragraphs the author paints a complete picture of the white wines of the region: "White wines from the river banks are called *vins de primeur*, and this name is frequently used in error for sweet wines. The *vins de primeur* are wines which are bought and transported at the beginning of the season, just after harvesting. They are, namely, wines from Blaye, Bourg, Cubzac and Fronsac which are transported to Brittany and certain other places. These wines are sweet and rich only inasmuch as they have just been made and are still unfermented. A fortnight later, they lose their richness. Some of the wines from Entre-deux-Mers are similar, although the growers try as far as possible to harvest in several stages, picking only fully ripe grapes. In some years favourable weather guarantees the success of this practice, but it is rather rare. Above Cadillac, for

example in Loupiac and Sainte-Croix-du-Mont, there are also *vins de primeur* which retain their highly agreeable sweetness rather better; these wines sell better than the former.

"Much further upstream, in places such as Aiguillon, Port-Sainte-Marie and Clairac, the wines are sweet, but their richness is less intense and rather better.

"The white wines from the Dordogne, such as those of Sainte-Foy or Bergerac, are *vins de primeur*. They are truly sweet wines with a powerful aroma and a sweet, intense flavour. They are wines from

▲ *With its gentle slopes and undulations, the landscape gives the impression of being in constant, gentle movement.*

the river banks. They are often accused of being blended and mixed with a sugar concentrate. Of all the sweet wines, it is undoubtedly those from Barsac, Preignac and Langon whose sweetness is outstanding, in that they not only have tremendous intensity but that it remains and even increases with the passing of time. These are not *vins de primeur*, that is to say that they are not sold in the early spring, either because they have been harvested late or because they are maturing in the cellars, and their price will increase after ageing. This wine, which can be kept for twenty to thirty years, equals or even excels the wines of Spain, the Canaries and Malaga, and is called 'wine of late autumn' *(vin de l'arrière-saison)*, just like all those which are sold only in March or later."

There are many important points to be noted in this text. We see that there was a desire for high quality sweet wines which could be laid down. We find the idea of harvesting in stages until late in the season. We see that the wines improve with ageing, particularly those of Sauternes which are considered as a class apart, and are rated above their counterparts in Aquitaine. And we note that these observations were not made yesterday! And to give the lie definitively to those who still maintain that the sweet wines of Sauternes did not exist before the middle of the nineteenth century, here is a quotation from Jullien, taken from his *Topographie de tous les vignobles connus*, published in 1816 (I have kept the original spelling of the various names): "The vineyards which produce the best semi-sweet white wines are those of Sauterne, Barsac, Preignac and Beaumes, situated on the left bank of the Garonne.

"Sauterne, a canton of Langon, some nine miles from Bazas, gives wines which are very mellow, spirituous, of great finesse, with a highly agreeable sappy aroma and a charming bouquet. The most famous are Clos Duroy, Ycum-Salus and Clos Fillot. Although their wines are all sold at the same price, the connoisseurs of the region draw fine distinctions between them and rate them in the order I have quoted. Barsac is a canton of Podensac, some nineteen miles from Bordeaux. The wines from these vineyards, and in particular from the area called Upper Barsac, are of the same type and sell at the same price as those of Sauterne. They are different in that they have slightly less finesse and bouquet and are less sappy, but they are more alcoholic, so much so that the wines made in years whose temperature has been favourable to the vines can be ignited as readily as can eau-de-vie. The wines of Barsac generally tend to take on an amber hue as they age. Among these vineyards, there is also a *cru* called Fillot whose products are of the first order.

"Preignac, a canton of Podensac, lies some twenty miles from Bordeaux: wines are made here which have all the qualities of Barsac and Sauterne; they more closely resemble the latter, from which they differ in that they are less sappy and alcoholic than the first. Beaumes, a neighbour of Sauterne and Barsac, produces wines which have the same quality and flavour as those from these two areas."

▲ *Ambassadors for France, the wines of Sauternes and Barsac have long been considered unique au monde.*

When Jullien speaks of "semi-sweet" wines, he means the wines of Sauternes and Barsac with their quite distinctive character, and he is careful not to equate them with what are commonly known as *vins de liqueur*, such as those from Alicante, Cyprus, Malaga and others such as Frontignan or Rivesaltes.

In 1839, Jouannet, a librarian in the city of Bordeaux, produced his weighty *Statistique du département de la Gironde*. With regard to white wines he wrote: "The harvesting period is not fixed at any definite date. In the cantons situated on the right bank of the Dordogne between Entre-deux-Mers, namely everywhere where the fruit of the vines is destined to be converted into eau-de-vie, red and white grapes are harvested at the same time, about September 25. However, even in these cantons there are some proprietors who because of the high quality of their grapes may make other use of them. These are harvested only as they are attacked by rot, and harvesting finishes considerably later. But it is especially in the great *crus* of Sauternes, Bommes, Barsac, Podensac and Preignac, well known for the excellence of their products, that picking is carried out in several stages. There the vines have often already lost all their leaves, yet are still laden with grapes. Moreover, harvesting is carried out with as much care as the Médoc gives to the harvesting of its own red wines."

This is one more example of established practice, established for generations in the viticultural traditions of the Sauternes region. When the Bordeaux oenologist Jean Laborde declared in 1907: "In the Sauternes region, the time when it became common practice to make wines with grapes attacked by noble rot can be dated to 1845", he was wrong, for he was relying on an entirely unverifiable tradition handed down by word of mouth with no text to support the claim. In 1850 Charles Cocks described the process clearly: "Speaking of harvesting in general, we have said that the pickers discard rotten grapes. This is true only for red wines. In the great *crus* of the white wines, all the rotten grapes are gathered with great care and, in order to have the ripest possible grapes, harvesting is retarded to such an extent that barely six weeks are sufficient to see the harvest through."

But what is certain is that from the middle of the nineteenth century onwards the producers of sweet white wines deliberately and systematically sought to obtain the effects brought about by botrytis. These effects were particularly noticeable in good years, and the wines of the great vintages became intensely concentrated. Such an intensity of sweetness led growers to encourage nature rather than to suffer its whims. And as time went by the men of Sauternes found themselves obliged to produce "Sauternes", whatever the cost and in good and bad years alike, according to a precise idea in the mind of the consumer as to the style of the wine. I am not sure that the "rationalization " of botrytis has actually improved the quality of ordinary, conventional Sauternes. Moreover, it is clear that the *Grands Crus* which respect their name and product use their label both selectively and sparingly (Yquem, for example, gives its name to barely 50% of its average production). This does not mean that wines now considered as not being typical of Sauternes should be condemned as worthless. It simply means that the idea of origin has become blurred in favour of the "style" of the product. This is a dangerous departure, for if pushed to its logical conclusion, it could mean that genuine Sauternes can be made in regions other than Sauternes, provided that it conforms to this recognized type. Indeed for a century or so, we have seen the growth in production of "Sauternes" from Australia, California, the Caucasus or even the Cape in South Africa. If you look in an English dictionary, you may read "**Sauterne** (with or without an 's'): Sweet white wine". And that is all. No mention of where it comes from. The flexibility – if not to say the laxity – of current French legislation means that it is totally incapable of guaranteeing the authenticity of Sauternes. One thing and one thing only, namely the growers' collective conscience, can preserve the style by which the wines are traditionally recognized.

I keep coming back to the term "noble rot". It is quite modern, going no further back than the last quarter of the previous century. It seems to have been invented by the clergy, who came out in a rash at the very word "rot". It should not be forgotten that the church was an important consumer of sweet wines. And it was difficult for society ladies and dandies of the nineteenth century to admit that such a divine potion could be the product of rotten fruit. The adjective "saprian" had already been forgotten. The ennobling of the term rot thus allowed fastidious people to pamper their taste buds without any qualms. In recent years, a scientific element has crept in to modify this concept. The term "noble rot" is tending to disappear, giving way to *botrytis* which, formerly used only in scientific glossaries, is the crucial factor responsible for the "nectarization" (I have recently actually heard this neologism) of the wines of Barsac and Sauternes.

But what is this botrytis known as the "rot" under the *ancien régime?*

Professor Bernard Pucheu-Planté (seen here) has carried out a series of scientific studies on the evolution of Botrytis cinerea. *Tiny brown spots appear on the grapes as they start to ripen. They develop slowly and prove that the grape has truly been attacked by the fungus. Grapes in the same bunch may or may not suffer from the rot (top right). This is the reason for staggered selective pickings. Bottom right: the cellular modification of the skin: unblemished on the left and attacked by botrytis on the right.*

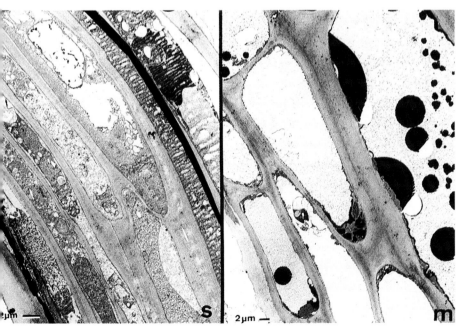

The noble rot:
its causes and effects

The word "rot" is not entirely applicable to grapes attacked by botrytis, for it defines the effects without describing the cause. Some writers have used the term "withering", which seems to me better, for rot is the pure and simple (or rather natural) decomposition of a dead organism, whereas the critical evolution of the grapes of Sauternes is a modification of their biochemical equilibrium by the action of a parasitical fungus called *Botrytis cinerea*. It is not when it is dead that the grape rots. It is the attack of botrytis which transforms its original constituents and gives it the appearance of rotting. But although stifled its life continues, and therein lies the difference which resembles a miracle. Elsewhere, the same fungus or its near cousins wreak havoc. They are the harbingers of death and, if allowed, will quickly destroy an entire harvest. Here in Sauternes, and in a couple of other privileged places, the "rot", by some mysterious alchemy, brings about a progressive concentration of the grape's essential make-up (rather in the way that an engraving, successively reduced, makes a superb postage stamp). So we should not linger over the more unpleasant aspects of "botrytized" grapes. I am even tempted to say that they are "living mummies", for that is more or less the process that is taking place. Common rot feeds on dead matter, seeking out any grapes attacked by rain, hail, birds and even tractor tyres. The rot called "noble" concentrates its attentions on healthy grapes, round and plump and bronzed by the sun, but which have been softened by early morning mists from the Ciron, that lovely tributary of the Garonne, which make a Turkish bath for the sémillon grapes.

A mysterious alchemy, did I say? It is hard to know how to describe this extraordinary phenomenon: the term 'biological miracle' would be equally fitting. But after fifteen years spent in observing, measuring, weighing and comparing the manifestations of botrytis in the Sauternes region, Professor Bernard Pucheu-Planté, of Bordeaux's oenological research establishment, believes that it is no simple matter. He is tempted to relate the rate of growth of the botrytis to the quality of the wine produced. But his conclusion is guarded: "These observations on the contamination of the grapes underline the complexity of the relation between weather and plant, plant and parasite and all three together – weather-plant-parasite."

Botrytis cinerea is a parasite which lives in a symbiotic relationship with the grape. It is a microscopic fungus belonging to the ascomycetes family, which includes 1,600 genera and 12,000 species (including yeasts, ergot, morels and truffles, penicillium). Among this extremely numerous family there are inevitably good and bad members. For example, to a viticulturalist penicillium and aspergillus are pernicious. If they invade a vineyard the wine will have a musty taste and the resulting acetobacters will turn it into vinegar. All forms of common rot attack grapes in poor condition. Gérard Seguin and Bernard Pucheu-Planté have even shown that their harmful effects are more common and virulent on vines which have shallow roots. By contrast "the development of noble rot requires a water supply to the vines such as will not allow the grapes' skin to burst". Its development comes about only as a result of days when wet and dry periods alternate. And it is precisely in this context that the little River Ciron plays its part and, to a lesser extent, the Garonne. The morning mists which spread over the vineyards two or three hours after sunrise "stimulate the development of the fungus, whereas the hot sunny afternoons help the evaporation of water through the tufts of the *conidiophores* (the minute hairs which conduct the internal moisture out of the grape) and the now permeable skin". The concentration due to this evaporation can then reduce, by up to 50%, the initial water content. Ideally, the invasion of botrytis should also be helped by light showers alternating with dry periods. It is when they have no more moisture content that the grapes are harvested. The wind also helps to propagate the conidia (botrytis spores). To sum up: the excessive ripening of the grapes, once they have reached normal ripeness, depends essentially on the prevailing weather conditions. Between three to five weeks of optimum conditions are needed for a whole crop to reach this extreme maturity. And it is this which explains why great vintages are so rare.

Any single bunch of botrytized grapes will include grapes which are simply "ripe", grapes which are "full of rot", and "shrivelled" or "desiccated" grapes. These two last terms are often confused, and the people of Sauternes and scientists alike use them indiscrim-

Measurements taken	1979 vintage		1978 vintage	
	healthy grapes	grapes with botrytis	healthy grapes	grapes with botrytis
Weight of 100 berries (grams)	241	133	180	76
Amount of sugar (grams/litre)	199	342	236	340
Total acidity (meq/l) *	96	134	95	117
Tartaric acid (meq/l) *	90	77	90	81
Malic acid (meq/l) *	33	37	31	56
Gluconic acid (grams/litre)	traces	3.03	traces	2.70
Glycerol (grams/litre)	0.17	8.05	0.13	5.13

* milliequivalents per litre

inately. Logically it would be better to distinguish the shrivelled grapes, that is those concentrated by the action of botrytis, from the desiccated grapes, that is those which have simply dried up, the two conditions being able to exist side by side. In the years when botrytis does not develop because of excessive dryness, the grapes become concentrated by desiccation alone. The wines which come from them have the traditional alcohol/sugar balance of Sauternes wines, but their aromatic character and flavour do not have that fullness or power of "botrytized" wines. In fact the terms "shrivelled" and "desiccated" complement each other in a very subtle way. For the effect of noble rot is to concentrate not only the sugars but also the natural acids, as well as the level of glycerol.

Bernard Pucheu-Planté has carried out rigorous comparisons between different vintages. His findings for 1978 and 1979, for example, are shown in the table above. Here we can see the very considerable evolution of the organic chemistry of the grape: 1979 was a year when botrytis developed well, whereas 1978 was a very dry year and desiccation was more common than botrytis. It is interesting to note the following points:
– the greater loss of weight in 1978;
– the greater gain in sugar in 1979;
– the stronger concentration of acidity in 1979;
– the greater gain in malic acid in 1978;
– the greater gain in glycerol in 1978.

Here I think it would be useful to make a short digression – but one whose main thread will lead us back to the heart of the present subject. I met Gérard Seguin for the first time in 1969, at the time 31 when he was preparing his thesis on the ways in which vines are supplied with water, a work which has commanded universal respect and which has since been followed up by numerous research papers. Together we strolled through vineyards in Margaux and I believe I can truthfully say that our knowledge was mutually enriched by an exchange of observations and ideas. He was a brilliant scholar, and I a failed peasant of sorts, but close to the earth and with my roots deep within it.

I remember a remark he made which to me was a revelation: "More than any other plant, the vine is a still which distils water from the soil by means of an apparatus which is at once very simple and very complex, namely: the nature of the soil, water from above and below, and the sun, the source of heat, all three playing their role in the life of the vine rather like sprites, sometimes kindly, sometimes malicious." This simplification is brilliant. It contains and summarizes the extraordinary life of the vine and the magical birth of the grape. Some twenty years later, I think I have remembered his words more or less exactly, I am happy to reproduce them here; and à propos of the present subject, I think I can extend the proposition by saying that in order to make good (or even very good) wine, this distillation is vital, but to make real Barsac or Sauternes *a double distillation is necessary*, each of the very best quality. The first is part of the classic life-cycle life of the plant. The vine draws up water from the subsoil and, at the end of the agricultural year, bears fruit which has ripened more or less well depending on the conditions of its production. We have seen that a vine which has deep roots "distils" the best grapes. They will be less sensitive to common rot; accordingly they will come from terrain suitable for noble rot, provided it is guaranteed favourable conditions in which to develop. Then the second distillation takes place, which transforms maturity into excessive maturity. Botrytis is an agent which guarantees natural concentration through its conidiophores. They act as tiny drains, discharging a considerable proportion of the grape's water content into the atmosphere, in a process quite as astonishing as photosynthesis, carnivorous plants or penicillin!

Refering back to the statistics given by Bernard Pucheu-Planté, I would like to suggest a convincing comparison requiring only careful analysis. This comparison covers a period of eleven years and is quite clear. I have deliberately exaggerated the scale to underline the differences between one vintage and another as regards the potential quality of the final product. The table which follows casts a scientific eye (not nose or palate) on the results of the "second distillation".

It is particularly to be noted that the grapes' loss of weight is proportionate to the success of the vintage, with the exception of 1977 which is notable for its lack of sugar and excessive acidity. Excessive? Yes, for as far as the present subject is concerned, everything is a question of balance between the different forces present in the grape.

We shall now restore to nose and palate the place they rightly occupy by calling on that great authority on oenology, Professor Emile Peynaud. In his book *Le Goût du Vin*, he explains:

"The balance of savours in white wines.

"The richer a wine is in sugar, the greater its alcoholic degree must be for it to be in harmonious balance. The sweetness of the sugar should be compensated for by greater warmth and vinosity. The lack of balance in little white wines which seem too sweet for their degree of alcohol is explained in this way: the sweet savour dominates all else. (...) Sweet white wines tolerate acidity better than wines without sugar. Thus at present, Sauternes has a total acidity of 4.5 to 5.0 grams. Either a lack of acidity or an excess of sugar will make these wines seem soft, syrupy and lacking in vigour. The impression left by a mellow wine should approach that of the grapes we eat. The mellowness softens the acidity and transforms it into freshness, and the slight stimulation of the acidity corrects the heaviness and the thickness of the sugars. So the aroma is enhanced by a felicitous interrelation of the elements, for it should be stressed once more that in this balance, the olfactory sensations have their role to play. The harmony of the structure is completed by the harmony of the odoriferous phase. An intense aroma, a very fine bouquet can mask potential structural faults, which are more apparent in wines which are weak in aroma and bouquet."

In order to illustrate his thesis, Emile Peynaud has provided an interesting diagram which is, however, rather sketchy. The expanded table which follows summarizes at a glance the need for balance in the wines of Sauternes. None of the basic components, alcohol, residual sugar and acidity, can develop by itself. The other two must increase in proportion for the triangle to remain equilateral, that is to say perfect. So a "half-sweet" wine will have a "half-alcohol", "half-acidity" and "half-sugar" content. It is the sugar content which determines the operation for it is the sugar which contains the potential alcohol; the higher the sugar level, the longer the other two sides of the triangle will have to be to accommodate it and maintain the balance.

33

Chemical composition of the musts from rotten grapes during the period of over-ripening (average of different plots in Barsac-Sauternes).

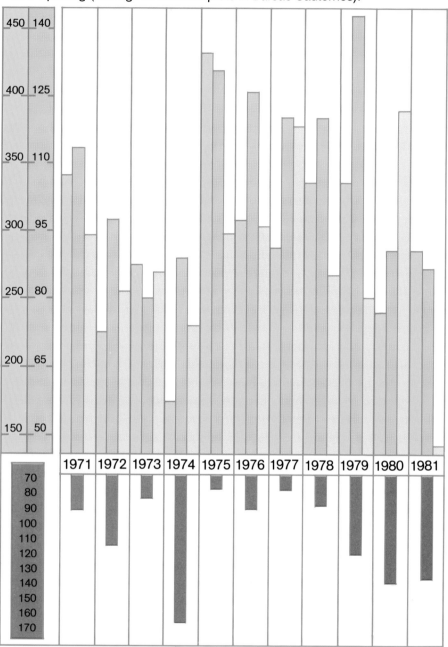

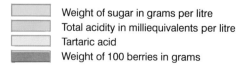

Weight of sugar in grams per litre
Total acidity in milliequivalents per litre
Tartaric acid
Weight of 100 berries in grams

I no longer remember – if I ever knew – who said (or wrote) that a great Sauternes wine represents "the extravagance of perfection". The picture below is valid in so far as the very best Sauternes wine possible can be represented by the largest equilateral triangle possible. From here on, descriptions have to be given in words.

The range of olfactory and gustative analogies possible with Sauternes is perhaps one of the widest. To draw a comparison with music, the registers and coloraturas are exceptionally rich. All the crystallized fruits in the world may be of service to those wishing to formulate their response in words. But there are also vegetable and mineral elements, from fern to tar, the scent of honey or elder,

or dried, salted and roasted almonds. The infinite palate of odours and savours of "saprian" wine requires an entire vocabulary, both for simple wine lovers and for scientific oenologists or distinguished gastronomic critics. But there is one trait which I find fundamental and which distinguishes at the outset the greatest Sauternes from all other wines. It is the smell of iodine. It can even be quite overpowering in the most outstanding vintages, when they have aged in the bottle for at least fifteen years. Yet it is always symptomatic of the unique and unbeatable "super-class" of the good *crus* in good years. No wine in the world can match it. No wine, cooked, baked, roasted, doctored, mulled, cooled or warmed, given a helping hand, macerated with anything, could ever have more subtle ethers. When the grapes have merely become desiccated, we find alcohol, sugar and a few principal odours. All well and good. But when botrytis has been at work and we smell the wine, we find a divine quality, diabolically accompanied by its slightly perverse volatile acidity and its light aroma of sulphur. Therein lies its genius. This, in short, is why the wines of Sauternes and Barsac are out of the ordinary, or even eccentric, we might say today, for they do not conform to any conventional pattern. Further on we shall speak at greater length of volatile acidity and sulphur. They have their critics, and it is true that in excess they are not easy to tolerate. Careful nuances are needed to make any judgement on a Sauternes. Everything is relative. A bull's-eye window in a chapel might well stand out dramatically from the solid wall in which it is set. But in a cathedral, it adds a discreet gleam of light which passes almost unnoticed amidst the dazzling stained glass, but provides an element of balance. Something which anywhere else would be a serious flaw, even a blemish, can become an embellishment. It is a question of proportion. Thus it is with the smell of iodine in great Sauternes wines. I think personally – and here, I led by instinct alone, I am venturing into an uncharted world of fleeting shadows – that this odour is based on the rather unpleasant smell of the magic mushroom from which it takes its vital force, its spontaneity, its bold originality and the qualities which linger afterwards: memory and presence.

For me, mere common mortal that I am, the smell of iodine has medicinal connotations: a convenient pretext for us to take Sauternes for medicinal reasons! The present state of medical research will not support the hypothesis that botrytis, once transformed into an antibiotic, has virtues which can be compared to those of penicillin. However, many relevant studies have recognized beneficial effects on the human organism from the wines of Barsac and Sauternes (as well as from those of Cérons, Loupiac and Sainte-Croix-du-Mont). It seems that the exceptional balance of alcohol-sugar-glycerol-botrytis makes up a high-quality nutrient with positive and powerful properties. Perhaps now is the moment for me to say a few words about this.

Bordeaux wines in general are good for the health. What is more, this has contributed considerably to their renown. But such claims are more often made in the context of great red wines, in particular those of the Médoc, nicknamed "old men's milk" or "invalids' wine". Readers may know the story of the man from Burgundy who came across one of his friends in a restaurant seated at a table in front of a half-bottle of Bordeaux. He exclaimed: "What! Drinking Bordeaux? Are you ill?" Whatever the case, for a long time now the medical profession has pronounced in favour of the consumption in moderation of Bordeaux wines. The late-lamented professor and senator Georges Portmann devoted the greater part of his career to proving this. In particular, he demonstrated that a moderate but constant consumption of the better *crus* lowers the cholesterol level. Few doctors have paid special attention to the effects of sweet Bordeaux wines. Thanks to the Perromat family, I have been able to read the thesis presented in 1911 in Bordeaux by Doctor Pierre Perromat of Cérons. His theme was "The white wines of Sauternes: a medical treatise on their alimentary and health-giving properties", and he showed that the glycerine in fine Sauternes is "not only an agent promoting digestion but a protective agent preventing indigestion, and a precious element in restoring invalids to health". A little further on, we learn that "the proportion of urea in the blood and urine decreases". As for the sugar in these sweet wines, he unequivocally declares that it is rapidly converted into energy, "almost immediately, which is very useful when a tired constitution needs to be restored rapidly, or whenever there is an anomaly in the normal metabolism, or when there is fatigue". Because of its ability to dissolve alimentary substances, alcohol promotes digestion. Pierre Perromat concludes: "Of these three elements, alcohol, sugar and glycerine, the one which can be used most rapidly by the cells and is the best nutrient for the muscles is sugar. Moreover, it is this which, combined with alcohol and glycerine and moderating their over-rapid action, gives the wines of Sauternes their beneficial, tonic and nutritious qualities."

The tailpiece which follows I find delightful: "The wines of Sauternes help respiration which they facilitate by acting on the inspiratory and expiratory muscles. The cardiac muscle is also stimulated and increases the number and amplitude of the heartbeats; so the circulation is accelerated. The muscles of the digestive and respiratory tracts and the heart are not the only ones to benefit from the salutary effects of the wines of Sauternes; they may be the first to make use of the wines' main constituents, but the other muscles also take their precious portion which they use to compensate for tiring exertions, the inevitable result of sumptuous dinners, speeches, dances, tennis, etc." I am now going to top up Dr Perromat's nourishing glass of Sauternes with a story from Maurice Chevalier. He once told me that when he was a young debutant in the music-halls, he would become literally transfixed with stage fright. His stomach seized up with cramps, his legs turned to water, his mind became a blank and his vocal chords became "as dry as the dust in the depths of the desert". After a long search, he finally found the perfect antidote to this malady, to which artists are notoriously prone: Sauternes. All he had to do was to sip one or two glasses of the "nectar of the Ciron" a quarter of an hour or so before going on stage to feel restored and back in fine form and fettle. One can picture our dear "Momo" raising his immortal boater for this final encomium: "I owe my success to the good wine of Sauternes."

And now let us return to Dr Perromat: "With the euphoric sensations they generally arouse, these wines engender feelings of benevolence, tenderness, affection, gaiety, cordiality, sprightliness, candour:

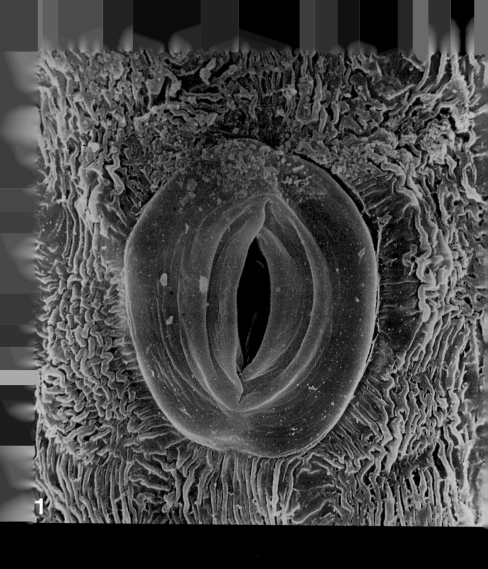

1

These extraordinary photographs were taken under an electron microscope by Michel Mercier (Bor-deaux I University) and Bernard Pucheu-Planté (oenological centre, Bordeaux II University). They show the development of botrytis cinerea. *Above, a young stoma of the grape skin: a natural organ-ism permitting respiration and exchange of gases. This microfissure will become a crack on excessive ripening. It will serve as a fixation and penetration point for* Botrytis cinerea *(2). Then it will de-velop more or less rapidly depending on weather conditions, thanks to the conidia (3) supported like berries by the conidiophores (4). Bottom right, we see a complete "botrytis unit", that is a stome and its peristomatic fissure with well developed botrytis and its yeasts.*

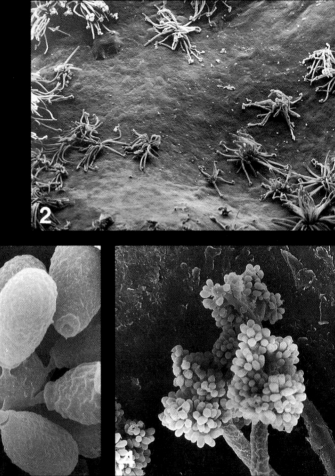

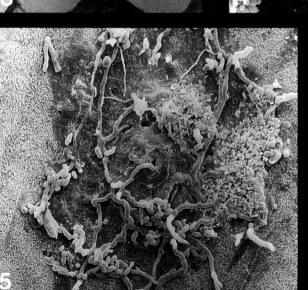

sentiments which together make for life's well-being and the charm of society. As the brain is affected, the effects develop. The sad man rejoices, his thoughts quicken, his imagination is fired; the reserved man bubbles over with words; the misanthrope becomes sociable, the miser is moved with impulses of generosity, and the coward is capable of feats of bravery." The dear doctor must himself have been in a state of slight euphoria when he wrote these lines, so bringing further proof to his thesis.

Among the virtues which he attributes to the wines of Sauternes, both physiological and psychological (and I will not draw up a complete list), there are two which he has only lightly touched on. The first is in the realm of homeopathy. I find his observations judicious and interesting. He writes as follows: "In the case of wine, something takes place which is analogous with the effects that can be observed, but not explained, in respect of certain natural mineral waters whose composition is also highly complex, for though they contain only traces of minerals, they have marvellous therapeutic properties which pharmaceutical doses ten and twenty times stronger are incapable of producing." In fact, the very subtle components of Sauternes can resemble the complex formulae of chemotherapy but in doses as great in effectiveness as they are tiny in quantity. Herein lies a whole field of scientific exploration, as yet hardly investigated at all. We should certainly consider – and with satisfaction, glass in hand – every serious proposal on this subject (for example – and why not? – the trace element content of Sauternes). The second virtue he mentions without drawing any further conclusions. However, incorporating my modest intuition into Perromat's prognosis, I should like to quote this passage from his thesis as one of the most important in his study: "And finally, let us not forget the considerable bactericidal power of the wines of the Sauternes region, a power which was particularly brought to light through experiments on Eberth's bacillus carried out by Sabrazès and Marcandier (1907) with the 1890 vintage of Cérons." As everyone should know, Eberth's bacillus is the typhoid germ. At the time when Dr Perromat was writing his thesis, the German bacteriologist Karl Eberth was gaining medical renown after isolating and describing the bacillus which bears his name. The topicality of his research therefore certainly ensured the young Bordeaux doctor a favourable hearing. He ascribes the "considerable bactericidal power" of Sauternes wines to the numerous acids which they contain.

Acids can certainly have an antiseptic effect, but antibiotic? If it were so, Sauternes wines would not be so very different from all the

Maurice Chevalier was a fervent admirer of the great wines of Bordeaux and in particular of Sauternes. In the bottom photograph, taken at the beginning of the '60s, is a distinguished cross-section of representatives of the Bordeaux wine world (at a tasting in London). Seated, from left to right: Seymour Weller (Haut-Brion), Madame Daniel Lawton, Madame Pierre Chauvot, Madame Edmond Rolland, Pierre Chauvot (wine broker), Yves Rozès (ports), Daniel Lawton (wine broker). Standing: a director of the firm of Lebègue, Comte Hubert de Beaumont (Latour), Madeleine Decure (Revue Cuisine et Vins de France), the Marquis Bertrand de Lur Saluces (Yquem), Edmond Rolland (Coutet), a merchant from Burgundy and Pierre Ginestet (Margaux). 41

others in their "considerable bactericidal power". Now, one single fundamental phenomenon distinguishes Sauternes from other wines: *Botrytis cinerea*. So it must be to this, and to this alone, that any therapeutic properties of this sort should be ascribed. The antibiotics produced by *Botrytis cinerea* are called "botryticines". Their effects on the fermentation and stabilization of wines, that is their primary and secondary effects on the product itself, are now quite well known. But their biological influence on the human organism is as yet not clearly ascertained. Perhaps in a few years' time we will see "botrytized" wines available on prescription.

I shall now bring this chapter to a close, but not without drawing attention to another extraordinary property of Sauternes. Doctor Perromat did not dare to tackle this aspect directly in his thesis, but slipped it in among several subsidiary clinical observations. He quotes the case of a patient called François L..., a great drinker of white wine, especially keen on sweet wines. "On finishing his military service, L... worked for the wine compagny R... and M... in a cellar housing only *premier cru* wines of Sauternes and Preignac. The value of these great white wines did not deter him. On the contrary, profiting from this unique opportunity, he increased his daily dose and finally reached the average of six litres, of which five were of Sauternes (...) In 1904, as a broker with the firm of M... and Co., he was sent to supervise a cellar in Barsac belonging to the firm. Having little to do and with no particular pastime to while away the time, he took advantage of the opportunity of tasting the heady wines of the area and for three years he was in a constant state of semi-drunkenness. In 1907, at the Naval Exhibition in Bordeaux, he demonstrated the duties and functions of the Customs and Excise authorities concerning bottled wines. Having his tent close to that of Sauternes, he did not fail to visit it, and for six months there was no taster more conscientious than he." The medical report, as transcribed, also gives us the medical history of the subject; his general state seemed satisfactory: lungs, cardio-vascular system, gastrointestinal functions, reflexes and mobility, mental faculties, sensory organs, etc. When it comes to the urogenital system, the report becomes positively explosive: "L... is subject to excessive genital excitement with erotic tendencies. The fact of finding himself near women, in crowds, on the platform of trams, etc., the sight of women's clothing or objects serving for their toilet, perfumes, etc., puts him in a state of physical excitement, although he never gives way to unbecoming acts or misdemeanours. This genital erethism is particularly strong in the evening when he retires to bed, taking the form of an

intense priapism. Obliged to get up, he goes to copulate, then with a bottle of white wine in his pocket and driven almost despite himself, he walks for several miles. Returning home at ten o'clock, he then sleeps perfectly until about five in the morning. Once again in a state of erection, the cycle begins again and this takes place several times during the day, except when he is working." And, after a few related remarks, the doctor adds: "L... does not complain of the erotic tendencies which he presents. On the contrary, he is delighted thereby. As for his priapism, he is proud of it. His fleeting impulses have disappeared; his insomnia gives way after a few minutes of jogging. Only his mania for walking is inconvenient; although it enables him to know the area better."

So then, dear reader and lover of sweet great *crus*: now you know what other excesses lie in store if one indulges to excess in the wines of Sauternes! Etymologists claim that the French interjection "sapristi!" is a corruption of the word "sacristy". No such thing: "Sapristi" can come only from *saprien*. Good grief!

▲ *The "noble" rot (*Botrytis cinerea*) should not be confused with common grey rot which is purely destructive.*

Geography, geology, climatology, agronomy

The Sauternes region is situated approximately 25 miles upstream from Bordeaux along the Garonne. It is traversed from south to north by the Ciron, a modest tributary flowing from the Landes. The influence of this little river plays a decisive role in the excessive ripening of the grapes by *Botrytis cinerea*. In this respect it could be said of the Ciron that it is chiefly responsible for the Sauternes phenomenon, not only through the nocturnal or early morning mists which shroud the vineyards, but also through its role as a central conduit for the land, a sort of general collector of subterranean surface waters. The mists are the result of a simple phenomenon. The Ciron and the streams which aliment it along its course come, as we have seen, from the Landes. When these waters arrive at the Garonne they are relatively cold, for along their course they have been shaded by the great forests of the Landes. Arriving in the Sauternes region, between Bommes and Pujols-sur-Ciron, the river widens as the pretty valley broadens out. The sudden resulting increase in temperature provokes considerable evaporation, condensing into mists and dew during the night. This hygrometric alternation between day and night is precisely the most favourable climatic rhythm (one might almost call it a sort of respiration) for the proliferation of botrytis. Formerly, up to the end of the last century, the Ciron had another economic role, for the transportation of wood from the Landes. Accordingly the port of Barsac, at the confluence of the Ciron and the Garonne, was the centre of considerable river traffic. The twofold presence of wine and wood also encouraged many artisan coopers to settle there. Although on a viticultural level the name of Sauternes

The Ciron and the streams which feed it come from the Landes, bringing refreshment and enchantment to the surrounding countryside. ▶

has gradually conquered the whole of the appellation, that of Barsac is historically much more important.

Ever anxious to shed the light of publicity on their deep roots in the world of vines, the people of the Sauternes region, and in their turn many writers, equate the official Sauternes AOC with the ancient royal bailiwick of Barsac. This is incorrect, for the bailiwick covered a much wider area, having jurisdiction over Barsac, Cérons, Preignac, Sauternes, Bommes and Pujols-sur-Ciron, whereas Fargues was attached to Langon. At the time of the appellation's confirmation, Cérons and Pujols-sur-Ciron were excluded from it and Fargues was admitted. The Marquis Bertrand de Lur Saluces played an important part in this reorganization of the boundaries, and whereas Fargues contains a *Premier Cru*, Château Rieussec, Cérons and Pujols have no *crus classés* at all. So the Sauternes *appellation d'origine contrôlée* includes four of the communes of the ancient royal bailiwick of Barsac: Barsac, Bommes, Preignac and Sauternes, plus the land of Fargues. Within this delimitation, Barsac has the peculiarity of having the right to its own *appellation contrôlée*. Its growers can declare their harvest as they please, either as "Sauternes" or as "Barsac", those of the other communes can declare only as "Sauternes". In other words, all Barsacs are Sauternes, but all Sauternes are not Barsacs.

Barsac-Sauternes represents 2,000 hectares of vines under production. The authorized legal yield is 25 hectolitres per hectare with a tolerance of up to 30 hectolitres. This figure is too high (without exception) when it is a question of aiming for the level of quality resulting from the action of noble rot. In fact, the maximum yield ought to be somewhere between 18 and 20 hectolitres per hectare. The *crus* which make every effort to obtain the best possible wine in the Sauternes tradition produce quantities per hectare varying between 9 and 15 hectolitres. This obviously explains the high price the wines command. It can be nearly four times greater than the price of great red *crus*, and is also burdened by the cost of harvesting in staggered selective pickings, using experienced workers, and of ageing the wine in casks of the best oak, renewed yearly for preference.

The minimum degree of alcohol is fixed at 12°.5. In practice, all botrytized Sauternes naturally exceed this figure. We shall see further on when we come to discuss vinification, that the potential alcohol of the third pressing can reach 25° when the harvest takes place in optimum conditions. The original text of the decree of September 30, 1936 relating to the Sauternes appellation stipulates:

"The only white wines which have the right to the Sauternes *appellation contrôlée* are those which, fulfilling the conditions hereinafter stated, have been harvested in the communes of Sauternes, Bommes, Fargues, Preignac and Barsac, excepting any plots situated on recent alluvial deposits, such as feature on the land chart in the appendix to the present decree, and those which, by local custom, are given over to forestry." Conditions relating to production are then laid down. They name specifically the authorized root-stocks: sémillon, sauvignon and muscadelle; the minimum sweetness, equivalent to 221 grams of natural sugar per litre (4 ounces per pint); and the max-

Crus classés of Sauternes
(in order of their official presentation in the classification of 1855)

Cru classé in 1855	Commune	Proprietors (in 1855)	Present name of the cru
1er Cru supérieur			
Yquem	Sauternes	Romain Bertrand de Lur-Saluces	Yquem
1ers Crus			
Latour-Blanche	Bommes	M. Focke	La Tour-Blanche
Peyraguey	Bommes	M. Lafaurie	Lafaurie-Peyraguey Clos Haut-Peyraguey
Vigneau	Bommes	Mme Vve de Rayne	Rayne-Vigneau
Suduiraut	Preignac	MM. Guillot	Suduiraut
Coutet	Barsac	Romain Bertrand de Lur Saluces	Coutet
Climens	Barsac	M. Lacoste	Climens
Bayle	Sauternes	M. Depons	Guiraud
Rieussec[1]	Sauternes	M. Maye	Rieussec
Rabeaud	Bommes	M. Deyme	Rabaud-Promis Sigalas-Rabaud
2e crus			
Mirat	Barsac	M. Meller	Myrat
Doisy	Barsac	M. Daëne	Doisy-Daëne Doisy-Dubroca Doisy-Védrines
Pexoto	Bommes	Mme Vve Lacoste	merged with Ch. Rabaud-Promis
Arche	Sauternes	M. Lafaurie	Arche
Filhot	Sauternes	Romain-Bertrand de Lur Saluces	Filhot
Broustet-Nérac	Barsac	M. Capdeville	Broustet Nérac
Caillou	Barsac	M. Saraute	Caillou
Suau	Barsac	M. Pedesclaux	Suau
Malle	Preignac	Henri de Lur Saluces	Malle
Romer[2]	Preignac	M. de La Myre-Mory	Romer
Lamothe	Sauternes	Mme Vve Baptiste	Lamothe Despujols Lamothe Guignard

[1] *Château Rieussec is in the commune of Fargues*
[2] *Château Romer is in the commune of Fargues*

imum yield, 25 hectolitres per hectare as from the fourth year after plantation. It is also specifically mentioned that the pruning of the vines should be controlled and that "vinification should be carried out with grapes which are over-ripe (botrytized), harvested in staggered selective pickings. Any deviation whatsoever, even within legal limits, will occasion the loss of the right to the *appellation contrôlée* for the wines on which it has been practised".

As is well known, the legislation concerning the *appellations d'origine contrôlées* endeavoured to link geography and technology in the same qualitative spirit. These two concepts which are equally important in themselves, can be considered inseparable and this is what French legislation has achieved. In this context it should not, however, be forgotten that the essential word is "origin". Viticultural geography is a matter first and foremost of geology (soil and subsoil), climate and hydrography. All the human disciplines are grafted on to this initial trilogy, from agronomy, which deals with agricultural practice (or rather viticultural in this case), to viniculture, which deals with production methods: the transformation and finishing of the product which will be called "wine".

If France does not protect the idea of origin sufficiently, it will export its methods with its wines. Examples of this are numerous: the names of Chablis, champagne, cognac, and so on. have already been debased, and Sauternes has now taken its place among these illustrious but plagiarized wines.

This is why I think it essential to give a basic geological definition to the land of the Sauternes region, and one that will not be subject to change as a result either of evolution in methods or of the whims of fashion. Here then is a timely study of the geology of the region, of the kind to be found in all the books of this series. Once again my friend Pierre Laville has been kind enough to undertake this worthy mission, with the assistance of Jacques Dubreuilh.

Summary of the terrain and soil in Sauternes and Barsac

Situated to the south of the outcrop of Sainte-Croix-du-Mont in the Ciron basin, the vine-growing soils of Barsac and Sauternes have developed in climatic and geomorphological environments clearly different from those of the surrounding Graves, with, however, an underlying geology similar to that found in the Graves de Bordeaux.

It is the superficial deposits which give these areas their particular geological character.

There are six areas in all, including four layers of alluvial terraces, which give the essential nature of the Sauternes region; a limestone bedrock which predominates around Barsac; and, most characteristic of all, a thin veneer of all these sediments comprising a silty colluvium, eroded from the alluvial deposits on the high nappe further south, mixed with the outlying eastern sands of the Landes. Not to be found in the Graves de Bordeaux, this superficial mantle is characteristic of the region south of Langon.

The distribution of these sediments is what differentiates the vineyard areas from their surroundings. The gravelly terraces are very patchy, and the limestone bedrock, which up to this point is only occasionally exposed, breaks out along the River Ciron. This condition is explained by the river's vigorous scouring of the Garonne alluvium during the last ice age.

The geology of the Sauternes region can be summed up in five words, gravelly terraces with superficial silts, and that of the Barsac region in six, limestone slopes grading into clay soils. However, this geological simplification should not disguise the complexity of the soils, for this veneer and the overlay of superficial deposits, lead to a diversity of cool, deep soils, often with an iron-pan in the Barsac region.

The higher of the two, the Sauternes vineyard, occupies the area between the Brion and the Ciron, two small rivers draining the Landes towards the Garonne; the Barsac vineyard is wedged between the Garonne and the Saint-Cricq and Hountette streams. Sauternes is a vineyard of gentle relief, with a wide variety of slopes and aspects, whose general exposure is towards the north. Barsac is a vineyard of very gentle slopes orientated rather towards the east. However, over and above these subtle differences, the two vineyards are also appreciably lower than the surrounding countryside. And this characteristic, combined with the climatic influences of the Atlantic and the Garonne, confers on them a humidity which gives rise to mists, cool soils and, probably, the noble rot, that true treasure of the viticulturalist.

P. Laville and J. Dubreuilh, geologists with the BRGM (Bureau de Recherches Géologiques et Minières)

*

One particular observation can be made about the Sauternes region which links the soil structure closely with the landscape. It is especially true at Barsac, where there are outcrops of the underlying

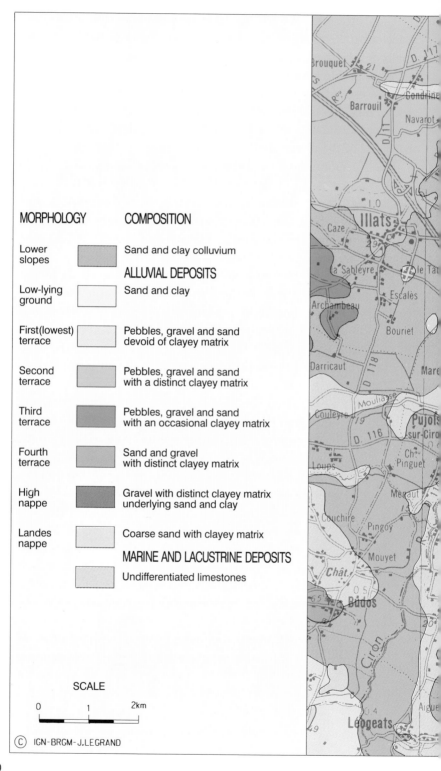

MORPHOLOGY   COMPOSITION

Lower
slopes   Sand and clay colluvium

                    ALLUVIAL DEPOSITS

Low-lying
ground   Sand and clay

First(lowest)   Pebbles, gravel and sand
terrace   devoid of clayey matrix

Second   Pebbles, gravel and sand
terrace   with a distinct clayey matrix

Third   Pebbles, gravel and sand
terrace   with an occasional clayey matrix

Fourth   Sand and gravel
terrace   with distinct clayey matrix

High   Gravel with distinct clayey matrix
nappe   underlying sand and clay

Landes   Coarse sand with clayey matrix
nappe

                    MARINE AND LACUSTRINE DEPOSITS

                    Undifferentiated limestones

SCALE

0   1   2km

© IGN-BRGM-J.LEGRAND

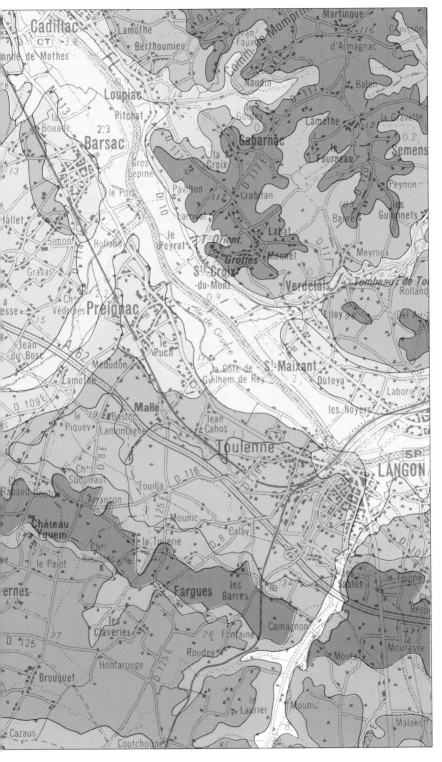

limestone, but it is also true of the other communes. If you take the tourist route round Sauternes, called the "circuit du Sauternais", all the roads will seem to you to be bordered by stone walls and for most of the time your view will be extremely limited. Several proprietor-growers boast that their estates are "walled round", and nearly all of them could say the same thing. Tradition has it that these walls were constructed to protect the harvest. This is to confuse cause and effect. For although the walls of Sauternes can deter stray fowl and grape thieves, the reason for their existence is the abundance of limestone at surface level. In order to ensure the best possible conditions for cultivation these blocks had to be removed from the land because they hindered ploughing. Rather than get rid of them, the growers preferred to use them to wall in their land. Barsac limestone is sufficiently "resistant and compact", according to Auguste Petit-Lafitte, to be used for building (indeed the villages round about are constructed with it). What gives the surrounding landscape its distinctive appearance is that the walls round the vineyards are on flat land. Generally speaking, it is on rocky hillsides that such networks of walls are to be found, where they serve at once to shore up the terraces and to support the slopes along which the winding roads run. In short, stone walls are more often found on hilly land. On plains and in valleys hedgerows tend to be used to establish boundaries. Although slightly undulating, the Sauternes region is nevertheless set apart by these boundary walls, which can often appear like a labyrinth to the traveller without a guide. Without subscribing to Taine's theories, I think that the morphology of the site has influenced the psychology of the local people. The inhabitants of the Sauternes region are highly individualistic. They do not know (or they feign not to know) what is going on "on the other side of the wall". They seem to be cut off from the world, even from their nearest neighbour. If the *grands crus classés* seem to be ivory towers, impenetrable from the outside, the majority of producers seem insular, each on his own land, each nurturing his own dose of botrytis. They do not even want to know if their neighbour has it or not.

Still in the context of geology, but in a rather more specialized field, this is the place to mention the Viscount de Roton's collection of precious stones at Rayne-Vigneau. It has been the subject of several scientific papers and remarkable samples from it are distributed among museums in France and throughout the world. Gabriel de Roton, who lived in the first half of this century, was a distinguished, erudite and enquiring man who spent his life cultivating his mind at the same time as his sémillon vines. A Hellenist, journalist and min-

The Vicomte de Roton's collection of minerals at Château Rayne-Vigneau is one of the most extraordinary in existence. As well as many curious fossils, there are semi-precious stones in great variety: zoned, banded and crystalline agates, quartz and rock crystal, jaspers, white sapphires, golden yellow topaz, lydites, calcites, aragonites, chalcedonyx, and many more. Many specimens are now in museums both within France and abroad.

eralogist, he earned the soubriquet of "prince of nectar and gems". His per name was a palindrome of his name, Notor, and he was given to signing his name "Roton-Notor", as if to lend his image some universal dimension after the school of Ying and Yang. But fortunately he did not take himself too seriously, and he could indulge in flights of fancy. Occasionally, his family suffered the consequences of this. None the less his collection, part of which slumbers in the drawers of Château Rayne-Vigneau, is worth mentioning as a curiosity of the Sauternes region. According to the man who found them, the gems came from a fairly restricted area: 20 hectares at most on a north-south axis. Several hypotheses have been put forward as to their origins, but no reasonable explanation has been accepted. The stones of Rayne-Vigneau are an example of the richness and the geological complexity of the Sauternes region. A detailed study of them would be welcome.

Without taking into account the Rayne-Vigneau gems, which they relegate more or less to the ranks of curiosities, Gérard Seguin and Bernard Pucheu-Planté are in agreement in recognizing the wide variety of soils and substrata in the Sauternes region and their complex composition. Men of science who also work with the soil, they have measured its microbiological and physico-chemical characteristics, together with its climatic evolution. They have to come to the conclusion that the Sauternes terrain has a specific character of its own which is accentuated by the particular climate of the region. "It is situated in the zone of the Atlantic climate known as Aquitanian. The average temperature for the month of January is 5.2 °C (41 °F) and that of July works out at around 20°C (68° F). Winter is generally wet. Frosts occur between November and April. The average annual rainfall is 34 inches." We cannot properly call this a "microclimate", for the term is nowadays used to describe a more restricted area. It is more a "climatic sub-zone" in which the communes of Cérons and Pujols-sur-Ciron could also be included. Moreover, these two areas also at times benefit from the same development of the botrytis fungus, which as we have seen is closely linked to climate.

One of the things the local growers fear most is hail. It follows a cyclical pattern: for a good ten years or so, its ravages have been less frequent. Following the terrible fire in the Landes which destroyed the northern forests of the department in 1948, there was a series of hailstorms in the Sauternes region for about fifteen years. The balance of air masses had doubtless been destroyed by the disappearance of thousands upon thousands of hectares of pine trees: a sobering lesson in ecology. Hailstorms in Sauternes are not a new phenomenon however. All the old records give details of their frequency and violence. Here, for example, is a report by François de Lamontaigne, a member of the Parlement (Société des bibliophiles de Guyenne, Bordeaux, 1926): "On Saturday, June 21 in the year 1760, around four o'clock in the afternoon, there was the worst storm in living memory over Langon on the Garonne. This storm came from the west and broke over different parishes, Noaillan, Leujats, Sauternes, Baume, Budos, Fargues, etc. The parish of Preignac fortunately escaped its devastating effects. For a good three-quarters of an hour, hail of an appalling nature fell, almost without rain, with hailstones as large as goose eggs. The vines were torn to pieces, especially in Sauternes, and particularly on the estate of Monsieur de Filhot, whose hopes of an abundant harvest were transformed in a trice into despair, with no hope of a harvest for three to four years because of the harm done to the vines by this hail. A child was killed by it; beasts too were killed and the roofs of houses shattered. Consternation reigned everywhere and peasants could be seen weeping on all sides to see this terrible scourge annihilate their modest resources." Though this cataclysm has yet to be repeated, hail is the great enemy feared by Sauternes growers, more so than frost, disease or pests.

Cultivation methods here, by and large, are the same as in the rest of the Gironde. The authorized varieties include, as we have already seen, sémillon, sauvignon and muscadelle. Several attempts have been made at one time or another with other varieties, notably riesling, but they did not give satisfactory results. At a much earlier date, red and white grapes were mixed in different proportions according to the *crus*. It is curious to note in Thomas Jefferson's *Travel Notes*, written in 1787, that "Sauternes is an unadulterated wine which, although made from grapes with red skins, is pale rose in colour for, being made without being pressed, the colouring matter of the skin does not mix with the juice." I suspect that this description is incomplete and partly erroneous.

First of all, one has to remember that it was common practice to plant black grape varieties among white and vice versa. In Sauternes and Barsac in the eighteenth century, white grapes predominated, though there were black as well. Both sorts were harvested and vinified together. Moreover, Gaston Galtier's French translation

(*La Viticulture de l'Europe occidentale à la veille de la Révolution française, d'après les notes de voyage de Thomas Jefferson*) does not exactly reproduce Jefferson's expression which read: "*Being made without pressure, the colouring matter of the skin does not mix with the juice.*" In my opinion, Jefferson meant that there was not any "intense pressure". The grapes were simply crushed underfoot, and afterwards what is today still called the "vin de goutte" was collected, this obviously being lightly coloured as it did not remain in contact with the skins for any length of time during the fermentation period.

The **sémillon** is a vine giving a very high yield, providing spring frosts do not attack its early growth. Its five-lobed leaves (which have a general tendency to appear three-lobed) are rather large, thick, pale green in colour on the upper surface and slightly downy on the underside. The budding period produces variegated leaflets. The stems are slightly flattened and mahogany in colour. The bunch is composed of tightly clustered round grapes, golden in colour and with a delicate flavour. The sémillon readily stands up to spur-pruning; we shall return to this later on.

The **sauvignon blanc** is relatively fruitful though rather vulnerable to faulty pollination. Its German equivalent is the *Feigentraube*, a word which means "fig-grape" and refers to the sweet flavour of the fruit, comparable to that of dried figs. It should also be noted that the sauvignon is relatively less subject to attack from botrytis than the sémillon, doubtless because of the greater thickness of its skin. Thus, the grapes of the sauvignon vine have a natural tendency to desiccate rather than to become botrytized. I am rather tempted to compare the German "fig-grape" with the *Passariae ficus* – the "dried figs" of the ancient Romans. The three-lobed leaves of the sauvignon are small, thick and a fine dark-green colour on the upper surface and downy on the underside. The stems are firm and burnt cinnamon in colour. Budding is uniform in colour. This vine likes pebbly, clayey light land, on a bed of limestone. It tends to ripen late. It is therefore well suited to the Sauternes terrain and can likewise be spur-pruned.

With its stability and sweetness, the **muscadelle** tempers whatever excessive vigour and aggressiveness the sauvignon and sémillon might have. It ripens early. It is also prey to faulty pollination and is highly sensitive to grey rot, which means that botrytis is not always successful with this stock. Its five-lobed leaves are large and thick, rather resembling those of the sémillon. Its stems are thick and less flattened off than the latter. Despite its name, its musky perfume is more an illusion than a reality. It is found in greater quantity in Monbazillac than in Sauternes. To wine made from a mixture of the three varieties it imparts its individual and distinctive personality, rather blowsy and common if its proportion is too high. A number of growers do not keep this variety in their vineyards any more because of its fragility and its aroma, which is rather like patchouli. In small quantities, however, it imparts an original touch to wine made from a blend of sémillon and sauvignon, which it completes in a rather coquettish style. My personal opinion is that it should not exceed a proportion of 5% of the varieties in any one vineyard. To give the best possible balance in order to make "great" Barsac or Sauternes wine, the proportions would be something like:

sémillon: 75%
sauvignon: 20%
muscadelle: 5%

This is a classic combination which suits the majority of the terrains in the region. But this is a matter of taste, if not of colour, although I shall shortly come on to the subject of "pale Sauternes", which is another story, begining with the pruning of the vines.

In a nutshell, there are two methods of pruning: long and short. The first tends to result in higher yields, often to the detriment of quality, whereas the second reduces the yield but thus improves the quality. Between "long" and "short" there are several permutations. The one thing which is certain, and which was already known by the time of Pliny the Elder, is that the vine needs to be pruned every year. In the volume in this series on Chablis, I have related the local legend of the donkey which, nibbling on a vine, became the original pruner. The folklore of Chablis has appropriated this story for itself, despite the fact that its true source is to be found in Ovid. In the first book of *Fasti* he recounts that one day a goat devoured all the branches of a vine, and like a good grower-to-be the witness of this crime prophesies: "Eat the vine's wood, piteous goat; but when the moment comes for you to be slain on the altar of sacrifice, doubt not that there will be wine enough still to sprinkle your horns!" And it should not be forgotten that in ancient Rome, the sacrifice of the goat was particularly dedicated to Bacchus.

Today a number of Sauternes growers row prune by the "single Guyot" system. The traditional method, used by the great *crus*, is is spur-pruning, in which all the wood of the previous year's growth is removed, retaining only two or three stumps cut very short, each bearing two or three eyes from which the fruit-bearing shoots of the new vintage will grow. In principle this practice should be universally succesful, for it fulfils one of the basic conditions required to achieve the highest quality. The extremely productive sémillon should be pruned in this way, according to the tried and tested practices of the appellation. But the sauvignon derives more benefits from the Guyot system. In practice this distinction is rarely made, each vine-grower adopting a single method for most of the time. Yquem is one of the exceptions. The sémillons are spur-pruned and the sauvignons are pruned by the "single Guyot" system. A vineyard using only the Guyot system risks overproduction, which means that its wines will very likely be "pale Sauternes". And let us not forget the old peasants' dictum: "To lengthen the vine is to age it; to cut it short is to give it new life."

*

Earlier, I mentioned Thomas Jefferson's *Travel Notes*, written just before the French Revolution. Since its first edition it has been widely referred to by many writers, for it sheds an enlightened light on the production of our vineyards two centuries ago. He was not the only one. At the same time as Jefferson was travelling through France, taking a particular interest in the vineyards, the English agri-culturalist Arthur Young was also engaged in a sort of study-tour of the French countryside. Jefferson displays great openness of mind and a good-natured curiosity which led him to record his findings with all the freshness of first discovery. Young is more thematic in his approach, seeking as he was an all-embracing philosophy which today might be called a political economy of the agricultural world. His work is therefore different from Jefferson's in both its conception and its direction. Young also takes a general interest in agriculture, its techniques, its yields and its potential profitability. When Jeffer-son comes to Sauternes, he lists the principal producers in order of their sale price, indulging in a few personal observations on the way, preferring for example "Sauterne to Preignac and then Barsac". But nowhere does he provide a treatise on viti-vinicological technology (except for champagne, whose production methods he describes). Arthur Young, on the other hand, always remains a specialist agri-culturalist. The comparison is entertaining. Jefferson visited Barsac

---

When the grapes are thoroughly attacked by botrytis, their skin takes on a pink colour
which often surprises the uninitiated observer. ▶

in about April 1787. On August 26 of the same year it was Young's turn. The latter does not expand on the quality of the wines but on the methods of ploughing: "...travelling through Barsac, also famous for its wines. Ploughing is carried out with oxen between the vine rows, a procedure which gave Jethro Tull the idea of weeding the cornfields with a horse-drawn hoe." This idea was the embryo of the famous "Tull system", then called "new cultivation", which came near to causing famine when applied to cereal crops. Bread and wine do not follow the same principles; nevertheless the eighteenth century Barsac was in the forefront of viticultural technology.

The heart of the wine,
from its birth to its dazzling zenith

Historically speaking, Barsac was probably the last of the communes of the Sauternes appellation to seek after wines which were essentially sweet. In the middle of the eighteenth century the wine of Barsac was described as a dry white. It was said to have a "flinty" odour engendered by the limestone subsoil, an aroma which the Maréchal de Richelieu, the last governor of the province of Guienne, compared with that of an old gun. Although the idea of sweet wine is, as we have already seen, much older than has been recently allowed, it is certain that the mellowness typical of Barsac and Sauternes today is the result of an evolution in the techniques of viticulture and vinification and a change in consumers' tastes. Which of these two factors came first? It is hard to say decisively, as no reliable sources give a definitive answer. The two tendencies have supported each other, with tastes developing along the same lines as technique. I believe the first great expansion in the production of sweet wines came about at the time of the Revolution. In its wake came troubles and famine resulting from such a radical change of "régime". I refer back to Doctor Perromat's investigations to emphasize the highly nutritious and energy-giving nature of the sugar content in a sweet wine. In times of scarcity, if bread is short, wine with a natural sugar content not only contributes to help balance nutrition, but is in itself a food. This observation is supported by the considerable increase in the demand for "sweet wines" in times of war, when there are restrictions. During the two world wars, the consumption of Sauternes increased significantly, as did that of wines from Loupiac and Sainte-Croix-du-Mont, Monbazillac, Banyuls, Roussillon, Frontignan and other slightly fortified wines. (As a result there was during both periods a leap in production of wines which were partially "manufactured", which greatly damaged the reputations of more authentic wines.) But let us return to technique. To define it, we must exclude everything which is not concerned with the period of harvesting: the whole period and not just the crucial moment when the fruit is ripe which, as for other red *crus* or dry whites, is decided at a single point in time. The expression "staggered selective pickings" has already been used enough for me not to need to elaborate here. And it is sufficiently self-explanatory for readers to understand what it entails in practice. Strictly speaking, gathering in the harvest in Sauternes is not a "harvest" but a series of "pickings". The word harvest conveys the idea of a general and systematic gathering, whereas "picking" has clearly to do with a manual and selective operation. As far as I am aware, no one has better described and explained this process than Richard Olney in his book on Château d'Yquem. Rather than paraphrase him, I prefer to quote his words verbatim, for I consider his explanation perfect:

"The dates and the hours of picking, weather permitting, and the condition of the grapes to be picked – the degree to which they are shrivelled by noble rot – are determined by the weight of the must, the level of sugar concentration.

Before the beginning of the vintage and repeatedly thoughout its duration, both in the waiting periods between *tries* and several times during the pressing of each batch of grapes, samples of the must are measured with a glucometer.

The appearance of the grapes, even when withered to the *rôti* stage, cannot accurately indicate their level of sugar concentration: grapes ripen every year (or nearly so), that is to say, they arrive at a stage of physiological maturity when, before advancing into various states of surmaturation from outside influences, the combined rising sugar content and descending acidity are arrested and, at the same time, the pips turn hard, deepening from a milky green colour to dark brown. But, depending on the season that has produced it, the sugar content of a grape that has reached complete physiological maturity can vary greatly. As it is this variable quantity of sugar that is subsequently partially consumed by the parasitic botrytis, the remainder being concentrated in the grape berries as they wither under the combined influences of the botrytis, the sun and the wind, it naturally follows that, from one year to another, grapes that exhibit visually the same surface effects of noble rot do not necessarily contain the same degree of concentration of sugar.

Harvesting by staggered selective pickings calls for great experience. The labour force is recruited from local people who have both patience and experience. ▶

In some years, only the individual grape berries that have arrived at the shrunken *rôti* stage may be picked to achieve the correct reading of potential alcohol; in others this concentration may be tempered by the addition of *pourris-pleins* grapes – those that are still plump but whose skins have turned brown; finally, following unusually hot summers and especially high potential alcohol readings, it may be necessary to pick a certain proportion of grapes unaffected by botrytis – *grains verts* – in order to lower the sugar concentration of a given *trie*.

Under no circumstances, however, must the grapes be picked when they are swollen with water from outside influences. Because the skins of grapes at the *rôti* stage have become fragile and porous, their structure broken down by the digestive action of the fungus, they and the dehydrated pulp act like sponges, greedily absorbing any humidity in the atmosphere. Rain will cause the withered grapes to swell with water and the sugar count will fall disastrously; sunny weather or dry winds are necessary to redehydrate them before they can be picked. Their thirst is quenched also by the morning mists and, even in perfect weather, the picking must wait until an hour or so of sun has evaporated the moisture which they have sponged up. The juice from grapes at the same stage of advancement, picked in the afternoon, often measures several degrees more potential alcohol than that of those picked in the morning".

In the edition of September 30, 1899 of the magazine *Le Vin de Bordeaux* we read: "Sauternes has begun its first picking, which has given musts weighing 24 to 26 degrees on the Baumé scale." I think this is a record. It is generally considered that excessive ripeness has reached its ultimate point at 25 degrees. The *Dictionnaire du Vin* explains how this takes place: "Picking is done with special scissors which enable the berries which have reached the required stage to be detached from the bunch in several runs or selective pickings. The first will be done only if the grapes are perfectly shrivelled and great care will be taken in selecting the berries. This picking will give but little wine; what it does produce is very sweet and is called *vin de tête* (first wine). The second run, whose yield is more plentiful, includes a mixture of rotten or *rôti* grapes in varying proportions, depending on the circumstances. The wines it gives may be classed with those of the preceding run or the following one, depending on the year. After these two runs come others whose harvest is made up of grapes which are in a state of more or less complete maturity or desiccation. The fifth or sixth run, which will usually be the last, consists of gathering whatever remains on the vines and, in the great *crus* and the good years, will form only a tiny fraction of the total harvest." The wines from these last runs are called *vins de queue* (last wines). Everyone has his own method of picking, and there are also different types of scissors. But the Sauternes area has its own gadgets and tricks. Some people use large hairpins, apparently the most efficient tool for picking berry by berry. It should not be supposed that the harvest will necessarily finish with the fifth or sixth run. Although fairly infrequent, there are still, even today, cases of greater numbers of runs: up to nine or even ten in extreme cases. A large number of runs does not mean that there is any difficulty in reaching excessive ripeness. It depends rather on the state of the harvest, the weather towards the end of the season and the considered decision of the grower.

As I have already mentioned, many producers make little or no distinction between shrivelled (*confit*) and desiccated (*rôti*) grapes, though the first should be gathered before the second. In fact it is very difficult to gauge the optimum degree of excessive ripeness. "The best way is by rule of thumb," as old M. Bureau, the former cellar master at Yquem, used to say. "It is the years of experience behind you which count." Up until now the proprietor or his right-hand men needed a great deal of experience to synchronize the pickings, while keeping a constant watch on quantity and quality, the weather, the cost of the harvest and the theoretical sale price of the wine. But quite recently a method has been developed for determining the condition of the grapes and calculating the level of activity of botrytis and the degree of contamination, though I wager that the majority of Sauternes growers are not yet familiar with it. The methods, developed by the firms of Sopra and Novoferment, uses a chronometric test to measure the sensitivity of the "Laccase enzyme", and from this at any given moment can give a precise reading of the present and potential condition of the grape. I do not know if this data is yet processed by computer, but a programme for this is certainly in the process of being written. In a few years, we shall have a data bank from which we will be able to calculate before Christmas every year if the vintage will be worthy to be drunk with the *foie gras* at Christmas and New Year ten years later! In the twenty-first century, Sauternes will perhaps be once again a "saprian" wine.

In the field of vinification, Ancient and Modern exist side by side. Here first of all is the traditional method: the harvest is crushed underfoot, then pressed rapidly without too much pressure. If the first run has been well done, there will be very few grape stalks and a preliminary removal of them will therefore hardly be necessary. Then 67 the compacted mass of grape-skins, the *marc*, is broken up either by hand or by machine to be pressed again and then yet again a third time. The first pressing gives 70% to 80% of the must. This is the best in quality as far as sensory assessments go but it does not extract the intense richness of the sugars. The second pressing gives about 10 to 25% of the total volume, depending on the intensity and duration of the pressure applied. The rest comes with the third pressing; this is the richest in sugar but can also extract unpleasant flavours from the grapes, which sometimes taint the must irreparably. Fermentation takes place directly in the cask. It develops slowly, particularly in great years. Botrytis generates a group of antibiotics, not well known even today, called *botryticines*. These slow down fermentation as the degree of alcohol increases. It is like a natural buffer, allowing the wine to achieve the balance between alcohol, sugar and acid described earlier. So, all in all, a great Sauternes wine will finally be composed of:

13 to 15 degrees of alcohol;

40 to 80 grams of sugar per litre (i.e. about 0.75 to 1.5 oz per pint);

4.5 to 5.5 grams of acidity per litre (i.e. about 0.08 to 0.10 oz per pint).

This three-fold balance is subject to a considerable number of variables.

To prevent or delay the action of the reducing sugars which tend to consume oxygen from the air, the classic practice is to use doses of sulphur in different solutions. If this is not done, the wine will oxidize very rapidly and take on a brownish colour (maderization) as well as an unpleasant bouquet and flavour. Judging the amount of sulphur needed requires long experience: the more the better, but only up to a certain point which will vary from year to year depending on the balance of the wine. With the passing of time, the sulphur combines, that it to say it loses its volatility and integrates finally with the liquid. This assimilation is best compensated for by extra doses so that the free sulphur dioxide still remains slightly positive. In old wines, an excess of combined sulphur dioxide can ruin the wine for drinking even though it may have a superb constitution. Generally speaking, for young wines, an initial nose of free sulphur dioxide fades away rapidly as soon as the wine becomes oxygenated on being poured into the glass. Excessive cold does not favour this evaporation. Sauternes wines should be drunk at a temperature of around 8 to 10°, that is, 46 to 50° F. Not less. Modern methods of vinification combine all the contemporary oenological methods as far as white wines are concerned. They call on equipment infinitely

more sophisticated than the primitive presses of our ancestors, and even of our fathers' time. Transistorized crushers-cum-destemmers, stainless steel vats which can be heated and cooled to order modern filters of every description, systems for separating the must from the deposit, or lees, before fermentation and clarification by cold treatment, etc., are all part of the panoply of the new model vintner. In the majority of cases (the exception confirming the rule), these instruments are used by the proponents of "pale Sauternes". I do not suppose I need to labour the point. In short, the wine-makers of Barsac and Sauternes can be divided into one of four categories:

the extreme classicists
the classicists
the new school
the well-intentioned oenologists

The first two categories prune their sémillon vines "by spurs". They perform at least three successive pickings. They vinify in new casks or in wooden barrels in which the wine remains for about two years before being bottled. It is golden yellow in colour and will intensify with age. The last two categories represent a broader viticultural approach with more generous yields. They harvest once or twice (by harvesting twice they maintain the tradition of several pickings) and

---

▲ *This collection of bottles of Yquem clearly illustrates the intensifying amber colour the wine takes on as it ages.*

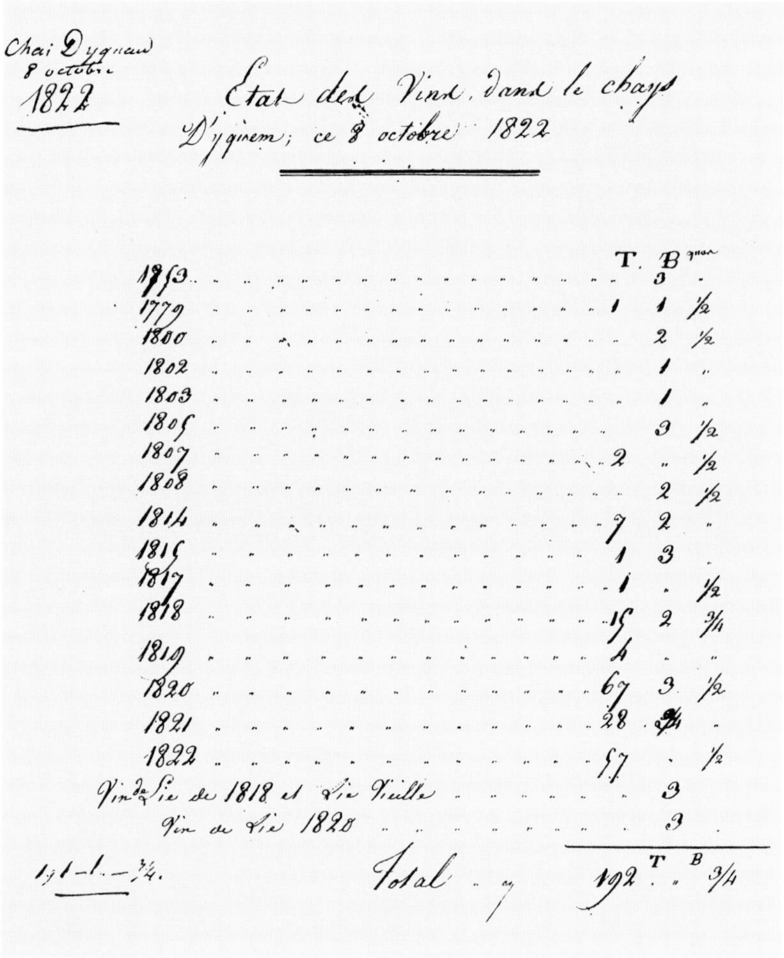

Chai D'yquem
8 octobre
1822

État des Vins dans le chays
D'yquem; ce 8 octobre 1822

	T.	B
1753		3
1779	1	1 ½
1800		2 ½
1802		1
1803		1
1805		3 ½
1807	2	½
1808		2 ½
1814	7	2
1815	1	3
1817	1	½
1818	15	2 ¾
1819	4	
1820	67	3 ½
1821	28	3¾
1822	57	½
Vin de Lie de 1818 et Lie Vieille		3
Vin de Lie 1820		3
	T	B
Total	192	3/4

salve their conscience by selling a certain proportion of beet-sugar
at the price of the Sauternes AOC (which is not unprofitable). But
they compensate for their nonconformist approach with maximum
use of technology which is efficient, hygienic and, let it be said, much
to the taste of the majority of today's consumers. These growers are
perhaps right to adapt themselves as best they can to the prevailing
market. However, they are drifting along a course I consider dangerous for the future of the Barsac and Sauternes appellations – even
if authoritative critics greet their products with elegantly colourless
phrases. For, and here I absolutely and solemnly insist on this crucial point for the last time, technology should be at the service of the
soil and not the reverse. Or else there is no earthly good in complain-
ing that the consumer is buying Chinese or Patagonian Sauternes,
which may also be the result of the best of contemporary knowhow.

I do not believe that *Botrytis cinerea* is a dying species. And were it to do so, it would be the fault of the consumer who, preferring not to know what it really costs the grower, refuses to pay the price for the finest quality.

In my book *La Bouillie bordelaise* (Paris, 1975), I relate the following story which my friend Jean Roureau, the late-lamented president of the firm of Eschenauer in Bordeaux, used to like to tell: "The management board of a highly reputable firm founded very many years ago was worried. Every year, sales were falling steadily. The chairman called in the very best consultant and explained the situation to him. In conclusion, he told him, 'I really do not understand at all. We make the best product by the best methods, with the best workers and the best material. So what evil spell has been cast on us?' The consultant asked, 'What do you actually produce?' The chairman replied, 'Horsedrawn carriages'. " This story is amusing but sad at the same time. I do not mean to imply that Sauternes is to wine as the carriage is to the motorcar. But I think that the consumer, or wine lover, and the producer, or grower, should both make an effort to meet more often. If the first is wrong in allowing his taste to stray towards the vulgar exoticism represented by cheap

▲ *A cellar in the eighteenth century (from the collection at Château Roumieu).*
◄ *An inventory of stocks in Yquem's cellar. It can be seen that wines were kept in wood over a period of sixty years.*

port (France is the world's largest importer of mediocre port), the second is to blame for not wanting to stand shoulder to shoulder with his colleagues to defend the image of Sauternes with irreproachable products and clear, unambiguous labels. For the health of the consumer, for the business prospects of the producer, for the survival of our culture, I raise a glass of Rayne-Vigneau 1945 (one of botrytis's sweethearts, as Pierre Louÿs would have said) to the hope that a collective conscience will exert its influence to save that common heritage bequeathed by our ancestors, and handed down from generation to generation from the time of Noah to the present day. Is this so difficult to understand?

*

In the book on Chablis in this series, I quote one of Professor Emile Peynaud's most telling observations. Speaking of the colour of white wines, which oenologists still have difficulty in explaining today, he said: "We should be able to recognize visually if a wine is dry or sweet." I found this proposition very interesting for, although I have never put it into words myself, it echoes my own sentiments perfectly. Two visual characteristics prove the professor right: the glycerol and the colour as such. In a classic Sauternes, botrytis, as we have seen earlier, is a concentrating agent for the glycerol whose "thick" presence can be detected at first glance as soon as the wine is poured into a glass and swirled round. "Tears" (also known in French as "legs", or *jambes*) form on the side of the glass, down which they glide slowly to the bottom. So the density of the liquid, its thickness and its unctuousness can be appreciated. There is no doubt here; this is the first consideration in appreciating a great sweet wine and it is the first criterion of its quality. The second is the colour. It should never be "white" in the sense of a modern white wine, rather "washy" with slight hints of green. It should rather be yellow, with tints of pale gold, and can even tend towards a deep gold or amber. This comes from the colour of the grape juice, not from that of the skin. For if the botrytis allows the evaporation of part of the water content of each berry, it also permits a greater penetration of oxygen from the air than in a "healthy" berry. In this way, oxidization already takes place before picking. Botrytis marks its presence and its action as if it were gilding the inside of the grapes, which it covers with its fine down. After this, nothing further is needed. The 'reducing' sugars are greedy for oxygen, whose slow combustion is successfully retarded by the sulphur. To use an analogy, if this combustion were intense the sugar would caramelize, so changing the colour. As a great Sauternes ages, it cannot escape from the progressive oxidation which we also call maderization. But once again, what could be thought of as a major defect in any other white wine here becomes an additional hallmark of authenticity. So you should never let yourself be put off by the sometimes deep colour of an old Barsac or Sauternes. One practical observation: sudden cold accelerates oxidization. Avoid chilling a bottle too suddenly by putting it in the freezing compartment of the refrigerator. An ice-bucket is infinitely preferable.

The difference between a golden Sauternes and a pale Sauternes stems from the fact that the first, unlike the second, is botrytized. Of course this is a sweeping statement. Between the two extremes there is always an infinite number of intermediary stages. And if I hail botrytized wines as the only true and great aristocrats of the Sauternes region, this is not to condemn the "pale Sauternes", which in their turn reflect a palpable evolution in methods and taste. In short, it is the difference between gold and silver.

Still on the subject of classic Sauternes for a moment, I would like to stress the need for ageing, firstly in wood, then in the bottle. I have never liked using the word "ageing" with regard to wines, as whether we like it nor not, it has overtones of decline and senility. I much prefer the term "maturing", which implies movement towards perfection. There are four stages along the road to the making and finishing of a Sauternes: over-ripeness, vinification, ageing in the wood and the waiting period in the bottle. We should not underestimate the importance of the last two. A good home-made jam will always be better after a time on the shelf, where its subtlest flavours will develop. And this is also the case for the great sweet wines of the classical school, which should harmonize all their constituent parts, allowing them to develop before revealing them, going through a sort of adolescence before maturity. Today the length of time for maturing in the cask or the barrel is of the order of eighteen months on average, more or less as in the Médoc. Formerly, it could be much longer and it was not uncommon for it to exceed five years.

Among other fascinating documents which he has inherited from his ancestors, the estate managers of Yquem, my friend Roland Garros showed me a stocklist of the château, drawn up in 1822, which includes sixteen vintages in barrel, the oldest being three casks from the year 1753, then sixty-nine years old! I should love to know (though, alas, I never will) what this old wine was like. Nowadays, 73

Five savoury dishes
for the lover of Sauternes

Fricassée of fish with Sauternes

Ingredients: *8 scallops, cleaned, 8 fillets of sole, each cut into three pieces, the flesh of 8 Dublin Bay prawns, 400g/12 to 13 oz. monkfish cleaned and cut into largish squares, a handful of shelled mussels, Sauternes or Barsac, fresh chervil, fresh cream. Method: Place all the ingredients together in a well-greased shallow pan, season with salt and white pepper. Half cover with a good Sauternes or Barsac. Add a few knobs of butter and cover with aluminium foil. Bring to the boil over a moderate heat and simmer gently for one to one and a half minutes. Drain the fish and arrange carefully on a serving dish. Add two tablespoonfuls of fresh cream to the remaining juice and reduce by a good third, adjusting the seasoning to taste. At the last minute add a few fronds of chervil and cover the fish with the sauce. Serve at once, piping hot.*

Recipe by Claude Darroze (Restaurant Claude Darroze, Langon. Tel: 56 63 00 48).

Tripe stew with cèpes and Sauternes

Cut of tripe and a calf's trotter and dice both tripe and trotter into pieces square. Cook for four hours in chicken stock, together with a bouquet garni and seasoning, over a low flame. Peel the tomatoes, removing the pips, and coarsely dice the carrots. In a separate saucepan, brown garlic, onions, shallots, chopped ham and sausage meat. Cook the heads and stalks of the mushrooms separately. When the tripe and trotter are cooked, drain and check the seasoning.
Put tripe and trotter in a deep earthenware pot or heavy-bottomed casserole, add the contents of the other saucepan, a bottle of good Sauternes and cover with the stock. Simmer the stew for about two hours over a low flame until it reduces by half. At the last minute, add the carrots and mushrooms.

Recipe by Jean-Pierre Xiradakis (La Tupina, Bordeaux. Tel: 56 91 56 37).

Foie gras with Sauternes

Steep a whole foie gras in brine to salt it. Remove the sinews and place in an earthenware cooking pot. Cover with Sauternes. Place in a bain-marie and cook very gently for about twenty minutes. The liver will be cooked when you can feel the heat in the centre of the pot, testing with your finger. Remove from the heat at once and leave it alone to cool for three hours. Drain off the Sauternes in which it has been cooked (this can be used again). Add a little fat from the cooking juices to insulate the liver from the air and keep it untouched for eight to ten days at a temperature of 4 ºC, 40 ºF. This enables the flavour to develop without harming the liver as is the case with port or other alcohols. The saved Sauternes will give even better results for two more livers.

Recipe by Jean-Marie Amat (Hauterive, Bouliac, near Bordeaux. Tel: 56 20 52 19).

Beef with Sauternes and Roquefort

Ingredients: *One tournedos (200g/6 to 8 oz per person), 1 table-spoon of Roquefort cheese, 1 glass of Sauternes, 1 glass of veal stock, shredded almonds, shallots and chives.* Method: *Sauté the beef, put to one side, deglaze and wipe the sauté pan; add shallots, chives and Sauternes and reduce until there is virtually no liquid left. Add the veal stock, reduce and add the Roquefort. To serve, Place the beef on the serving dish, cover with the sauce and sprinkle with almonds. Serve with steamed broccoli.*

Recipe by André Daguin (Hôtel de France, Auch. Tel: 62 05 00 44).

Stewed poultry with Sauternes

Take one boned wing and one boned leg of chicken. Beat them with a mallet to spread them out. Season. Prepare a stuffing with two tablespoonfuls of sausage-meat and a little foie gras. Spread this on one of the two pieces. Put a thin slice of foie gras in the middle. Cover with the other piece. Wrap in aluminium foil. Put this into a sauté pan with a good handful of button mushrooms, a glass of Sauternes and a teacupful of fresh cream. Start to cook over a high heat then place in the oven for ten minutes. Remove the foil and place the meat in the sauce. Allow to stew for twelve minutes. The sauce should bind by itself. To serve, place the meat on a serving dish, decorating with veal sweetbreads braised in Sauternes. A few button mushrooms can also be used for decoration.

Recipe by Pierre Bugat (La Réserve, Pessac L'Alouette. Tel: 56 07 13 28).

after the time spent in barrel, several years in bottle are needed for the wine to show itself at its best. The remarkable example of Christian Médeville, of Château Gilette in Preignac, who puts his wine on the market only after twenty years, deserves our acclaim. This patience is rewarded by a staggering olfactory and gustative harmony. But if we were to work out the true cost of such a product, taking into account the total financial outlay, the final bill might be hard to swallow!

On the other hand, "pale Sauternes" meets the demand for a wine which can be drunk soon after the harvest. These wines are not without their charm and make excellent aperitifs, for example, and luxurious sauces for cooking. This last use deserves special mention. The character of a Sauternes wine confers tremendous distinction on any recipe in which it is used. I could write a whole book of recipes using Sauternes. The majority of famous chefs have several. Obliged to make a selection, I have chosen the five delicious dishes on the previous page.

*

It is often said that contemporary gastronomy overlooks the wines of Barsac and Sauternes. This is especially true in France. The countries which are traditionally great consumers of wine are faithful (though in reduced quantities) to our great sweet wines. And there is also increasing interest among the Japanese (and, to a lesser extent, the Australians) in this type of wine. But it is true that eating habits and the average (and often ordinary) palate of the customer have, over a generation, removed Sauternes from everyday use, relegating it to the ranks of the exceptional, if not the bizarre. They are indeed exceptional wines. But above all drinking them is a question of habit. It is also true that for the celebration of any special event among friends, family or professionals, the idea of uncorking a few bottles of this liquid gold, yellow or pale, would rarely occur to people. And yet what a celebration it would be! And what quality, if the trouble is taken to choose well! As an aperitif, a glass of Sauternes is, for the palate, stomach and head, a delicacy infinitely superior to all other decoctions invented by man. One of the divine nectar's problems is that once the bottle has been opened you have to finish it (although a well-constructed Sauternes can remain "broached" for about twenty-four hours). But the same is true of champagne. I am quite prepared to recognize the lively virtues of champagne. But bubbles, more bubbles and still more bubbles! On the subject of uncorked Sauternes, I am reminded of little story about something which happened to me in Canada some twenty years ago. One fine Sunday in spring, I was invited to the house of some friends, beside themselves with excitement at the idea of receiving a guest from Bordeaux. They had laid on a great spread. As soon as I entered, I was assailed by a fine smell which filled the house. After the customary formalities, my host suggested I should take a glass; which of course I could not refuse to do. After a great parade of polite gentility, rather in the style of the eighteenth century, he served me a small amount of a liquor, deep oak in colour, poured from a white Bordeaux-shaped bottle into a sherry glass, elaborately engraved in the style of the Romantic period. I was surprised. He said to me: "Drink, my friend; I think I am giving you the best I have." I drank. It was curious. The potion was not lacking in character, but I had never drunk anything like it. I risked two words of comment: "How interesting". This was sufficient for the master of the house to feel more at ease. "Is it not? I have treasured this bottle with great care – as if it were a family jewel. I opened it in October last year with my wife and children to celebrate our wedding anniversary. Then we took another sip again on New Year's Day. It is a Château Suduiraut 1924. I was waiting for a grand occasion to finish it. I am delighted it should be with yourself!" How was I to react in the face of a demonstration of such kindness? Even today I am still touched by this warm gesture which was responsible for my tasting a Suduiraut 1924 some eight months after it was first uncorked. This memory prompts me to quote the Bible: "Reward cometh not from purpose of heart but from memory."

But we should not restrict the drinking of Sauternes to the aperitif hour. The late Marquis de Lur Saluces was a zealous proponent of good food companied by Sauternes:

"Must it be for ever repeated that Sauternes are not just simply 'dessert wines', as so many people tend to view them. These wines are delectable, certainly, both with ice-cream and almond flan, with *compôte* or fruit. But how much better with *foie gras,* or a delicate fish with a certain unctuousness accompanied by a rich butter or cream sauce, turbot with a *mousseline* sauce, pike *quenelles,* fillet of sole prepared in whatever way." Many wine lovers say that if you serve a sweet wine at the beginning of a meal, the red wines which follow will be massacred. I do not entirely agree with them. A pause and a glass of cold water will neutralize this impression. For me however, the undeniable glory of great Barsac or Sauternes is to be found

A few well-known Sauternes figures. Top: J. Comet owns vines which she has rented out; P. Lanneluc, grower, printer, inventor; B. Fage, Sauternes' sacristan (Domaine de Terrefort). Middle: A. Biarnès, cooper in Barsac, and his friends. Bottom: two unpretentious restaurants: "Le Sauternais" and "l'Auberge des vignes".

with Roquefort cheese (mould against mould) or any other cheese of this type. Not a great lover of desserts personally, I know no better delicacy than an excellent Roquefort spread in the hollow of celery stalks and savoured with a divine botrytized nectar. But chocolate cake, vacherin and apple tart also go well with it. Going backwards through the menu, and at the risk of being called a heretic, I would venture to say that Sauternes is the best white wine to accompany smoked salmon or pickled herrings. No other white wine, not even the greatest, is as long in the mouth. The classic marriage is vodka or aquavit. Sauternes is less brutal, infinitely more subtle.

Sauternes is not a wine to be used simply to wash down any dish, much less a meal. It is a delectable counterpoint of complementary, sometimes even conflicting savours. You do not drink Sauternes; you savour it by drops. The best way to appreciate an excellent Barsac or Sauternes is to drink it alone, accompanied perhaps, if you must, by a morsel of something delicate. But it is a wine which deserves your undivided concentration. In the evening after dinner, if you are wise enough to go without a dessert, open your barely chilled bottle and take the trouble to get to know it properly, to digest it thoroughly. I assure you that you will not regret the experience.

*

The traveller who wants to get to know the Sauternes area would be well advised to take a good road map with him. The map at the beginning of this book, based on the work of the National Geographical Institute map (as is the case for all the books in this collection), may also be useful in guiding you round the region. In fact I would say it is essential, for despite the number of signposts and notices, it is not always easy to find the road you are looking for and get where you want. But in summer, it is delightful to wander through the winding roads of the Sauternes area, bordered by mellow stone walls. And in autumn the gentle sunlight, soft and shimering bathes the countryside in its golden light, like André Chénier's *La Lampe*.

The traveller will visit the châteaux and cellars of his choice (by appointment preferably). He will take his time. In Sauternes no one likes to rush, following the leisurely pace set by the Ciron which, after the gorges of Préchac, winds lazily through the vineyards. It will be a journey through both time and space. Centuries will roll by, with pigeon lofts and churches, the façades of châteaux, each bearing the

date of its vintage from Pope Clement V to Napoleon III, and from every period of architecture from Louis XI to Louis XVI. With each stop, the traveller will step into the past, evocative of the historic tradition which the Commanderie du Bontemps de Sauternes-Barsac strives to bring to life again at its simple and dignified ceremonies. All the names which line the route and which appear on the world's most prestigious wine labels bear witness to a spirit of perfection rarely encountered in the history of man's endeavours, and all through the sovereign magic of a microscopic fungus called *Botrytis cinerea.*

Those who know the wines of Barsac and Sauternes also know a philosophy of life in which ecology joins hands with the art of living, hedonism meets temperance, the sublime moment is poignant in its transience.

The wines of Sauternes and Barsac are indeed "saprian" wines.

Catalogue
of crus

The proprietor of a *cru* situated in the commune of Barsac may, if he wishes, declare his harvest under either the Barsac or the Sauternes appellation. The growers in the other communes (Bommes, Fargues, Preignac and Sauternes) must all declare their harvest as AOC Sauternes.

Many growers in Barsac and Sauternes make dry white wines. A few of these may be mentioned in the catalogue under one entry or another, but no attempt has been made to give an exhaustive list of wines of this type.

The term *cru classé* is used only in describing the *crus* belonging to the official 1855 classification. The date is not repeated each time the classification is mentioned.

The number of coloured glasses beside a *cru* gives an idea of the value for money it represents. This estimation, while arrived at as objectively as possible, is naturally subject to discussion and to change. It is intended as a rough guide and has no official standing as a classification.

This symbol denotes an exceptional wine.

Certain châteaux have one or more different labels for other wines produced by the property (for example wines from young vines). Such wines are followed by an arrow which indicates the château of origin.

This symbol indicates that a particular name is the secondary wine of a larger estate.

This denotes château-bottled.

81

Alexandre de Lur Saluces (Comte)

Alexandre de Lur Saluces.

It may be unusual to use a Christian name to define a person's position in an alphabetical catalogue. But if Comte Alexandre de Lur Saluces had been called, for example, "Xavier" or "Yves", I should not have been able to use this excuse to place him right at the beginning of this section of the book. Inevitably, Château d'Yquem is to be found in its rightful place, that is at the very end of the catalogue. But I thought it fitting that, the king of Sauternes should be mentioned first. Today, Alexandre de Lur Saluces is at the head of this sumptuous *cru* to which he devotes himself entirely. The heir of the Marquis Bertrand de Lur Saluces (his uncle) is dedicated to family tradition. For Yquem, he may be considered as a sort of guardian of the temple. His wife, Bérengère, assists him with intelligence, charm and efficiency. Thanks to them, Yquem is not a fossil, but gives a vigorous, lively image to the finest white wine in the world.

Andoyse (Château) ⚬ → Romer du Hayot

Arche (Château d')

🍷 🍷 🍷 🍷 🍷

2e cru classé

Commune: Sauternes. **Proprietor:** Bastit Saint-Martin Heirs. Manager and director: Pierre Perromat. Cellar master: Serge Banchereau. Consultant oenologist: Chambre d'Agriculture oenological laboratory. **Size of vineyard:** 30 hectares. **Average age of vines:** 20 years **Varieties:** 10% sauvignon, 90% sémillon. **Production:** 60,000 bottles CB. **Visits:** weekdays from 8 a.m. to noon and 2 to 6 p.m. Serge Banchereau, tel. 56 63 66 55. **Direct sales:** Château d'Arche, Sauternes, 33210 Langon. **Retail sales.**

"Château d'Arche, formerly called *cru de Braneyre* and situated on the top of a hillside dominating the Ciron and the surrounding valleys, recalls an ancient family, several of whose members served with distinction in Parlement and on Guienne's Board of Excise from 1723 to 1789. A square, castellated tower standing at the west end of a rectangular building and several mouldings surrounding old lattice windows are the only vestiges which remain after the modifications of the last century." This is what Charles Dormontal has to say of this noble estate. It was created by the Comtes d'Arche at the beginning of the eighteenth century and it enjoyed a great reputation under the *ancien régime*. With the Revolution, the property was split up into several parcels which passed into the hands of the Dubourg, Lafaurie, Pentalier and Lacoste families. At that time, the names of those who owned any portion of the estate featured in the name of the *cru*. In 1855, Arche was not what it had

The square castellated tower of Château d'Arche dates from...

been a century earlier, which explains why it is classed among the second *crus*. Here we see what a chancy matter certain evaluations can be. For sometimes with each succeeding generation, such and such a vineyard can be of greater or lesser standing.

From 1860 to 1893, Château d'Arche was in the hands of Pierre Méricq, an enlightened grower who considerably increased the general reputation of the estate. Then came G. Dubédat, with part of the estate run by the Lafaurie heirs, and part of Château d'Arche-Vimeney held by the Lacoste family. In 1930, Armand Bastit Saint-Martin, the husband of one of the Dubourg daughters, bought the Pentaliers' share. Thirty years later, he managed to recover that of the Lafauries and to lease the little vineyard of Vimeney. So, nearly two centuries after the Comtes d'Arche, the property has been brought together under one wing again. Today it is Pierre

Perromat, the former president of the *Institut national des appellations d'origine* and

the days when its proprietors wore powdered wigs.

present president of the Caisse Régionale du Crédit Agricole, who runs the estate as a careful and conscientious tenant. But as a result of the Bastit Saint-Martin succession, the 4.5 hectares making up Arche-Vimeney have been sold to Cordier to be annexed by Lafaurie-Peyraguey.

The wine of Arche, as it is at the moment, is the result of a rigorous policy aimed at maintaining the most traditional Sauternes style. Pruning is done exclusively "by spurs" (no shoot is left too long). The natural concentration of the grapes is monitored daily and the yield is around 15 hectolitres per hectare. Harvesting is carried out in seven to ten runs. Fermentation is slow. Ageing in casks of new oak lasts between twenty and twenty-four months. And all this is consummated by a rigorous selection which retains only the very best. I believe that Château d'Arche deserves to be hailed as one of the best Sauternes of our day.

Arche-Pugneau (Cru d')

Commune: Preignac. **Proprietors:** Jean-Pierre Daney and his son, Francis Daney. Consultant oenologist: Pierre Sudraud. **Size of vineyard:** 13 hectares. **Average age of vines:** 30 to 50 years. **Varieties:** 72% sauvignon, 18% sémillon, 10% muscadelle. **Production:** 20 to 25 *tonneaux*, 10 to 15,000 bottles CB. **Visits:** Daily. Sundays by appointment. Jean-Pierre Daney, tel. 56 63 24 84. **Direct sales and by mail order:** in France. Jean-Pierre Daney, aux Charmilles, Preignac, 33210 Langon. **Retail sales.**

"With each changing year, the wine has its personality and every bottle develops, living out its own destiny." So says Jean-Pierre Daney, who has deliberately chosen – for almost philosophical reasons – to espouse finesse as opposed to the heavy geometric generosity of more monumental Sauternes. The *cru* has been in the family since 1923, after belonging to the Duthils and the captain of the frigate Latapy. Mainly situated in the area of Boutoc, it also scatters its different plots over the communes of Sauternes, Bommes, Barsac and, of course, Preignac. It is an old and highly respected name which Féret's editions of *Bordeaux et ses Vins* have always placed among the leading Preignac *crus*. Beyond all question, it is, together with Château Gilette, the finest quality to be found in this commune as far as the *crus classés* are concerned. Moreover, few other châteaux can offer themselves the luxury of four or five systematic pickings, light pressing with the help of a press which could well grace the window of an antique shop and ageing in the wood for three years.

The visitor will be well received all year round. If he wants to help with the harvest, he can see for himself the delicacy of the work. But if he wants to carry out a thorough investigation, he will need time. For the 1985 vintage, harvesting finished on November 18. And the result? I promised not to not reveal anything before the wine was bottled. Now, I can reveal that the princely wine of Yquem itself could well be surprised.

In the cellars of d'Arche-Pugneau, the tasting table stands ready.

Armajan des Ormes (Château d')

Commune: Preignac. **Proprietor:** Madame M. Perromat. Consultant oenologist: C.E.I.OE. in Cadillac. **Size of vineyard:** 9.25 hectares. **Average age of vines:** 30 years. **Varieties:** 30% sauvignon, 60% sémillon, 10% muscadelle. **Production:** 25 *tonneaux*, 12,000 bottles CB. **Visits:** strictly by appointment. M. Perromat, tel. 56 63 22 17. **Direct sales and by mail order:** in France and abroad. Château d'Armajan, Preignac, 33210 Langon. **Retail sales:** through local merchants.

At the beginning of this century, Jean Barennes was a palaeographer whose learning was equalled by his talent as a writer. He has left us several works of outstanding quality, the most famous being *Viticulture and Vinification in Bordeaux in the Middle Ages*. Vineyard owners often used to call on him to shed light on the dark corners of history, just as Professor René Pijassou does today or as Henri Enjalbert did not so long ago. Thus it was that in 1920 he published a *Notice historique* concerning Château d'Armajan des Ormes: "The château and the holdings surrounding it represent a large estate, the centre of a vast agricultural undertaking, whose seigniorial origins are at once obvious. Closer study confirms this first impression. This is no house of cards hastily constructed and likely to fall rapidly into ruin. It deserves to be included among the interesting monuments of the Bordeaux region as much for

Armajan des Ormes has received Catherine de Medici.

the noble history of its owners as for its archaeological and architectural features."
He also gives details concerning the proprietors of former times. Noting that the
seigniorial origin of this land goes back to the Sauvage family, who have been in
the Langon region since the fourteenth century. In 1565, Catherine de Medici and
her son, King Charles IX, stayed at Armajan. An inscription on the pediment of
the main door records the conferring of a title on Pierre Sauvage. The latter seems
to have been a notable figure in the area. His will indicates a huge fortune as well
as showing his generosity towards the poor. After disinheriting his youngest son
and his six daughters, he bequeathed Armajan to Pierre de Sauvage, his eldest son.
As a result of family strife, the feudal benefice then passed to the Arnaux and the
Guichaners, well-to-do Bordeaux families who provided the Parlement with several
magistrates. In the eighteenth century, Vincent de Guichaner married Marie de
Secondat, the daughter of Montesquieu. After the Revolution, the fate of the estate
becomes somewhat confused. We know that for a time it belonged to "Fiton, a
barrique-maker", then, during the nineteenth century, it was split up and fell successively to the Appiaus, Delbourgs and Lamarques. On October 31, 1846, the Duc
de Montpensier (Louis-Philippe's son) and his wife spent the night there in order
to watch the harvest. In 1912 a new proprietor, Armand Gallice, entirely restored
the vineyard, by then devastated by mildew and phylloxera and, made the château
habitable again.

   Since 1953, the estate has been in the hands of the Perromat family, famous republican landowners of the Garonne who are to be found on both sides of the river.
Madame Perromat-Machy currently signs the label of the *cru* "vinified according to
the best traditions", as Féret the Prophet has it. This name, one of the oldest and
most historic of the Sauternes region, merits more publicity especially in view of
the quality of recent vintages.

Arnaudas (Château) ⚱ → *Rolland*

Arrançon (Cru d') ou Cru du Violet   ♟ ♟ ♟ ♟ ♟

Commune: Preignac. **Proprietor:** Jean Taudin. Directors,
estate and vineyard managers: M. Taudin and his son.
Size of vineyard: 4 hectares. **Average age of vines:** 30 years.
Varieties: 15% sauvignon, 70% sémillon, 15% muscadelle.
Production: 8 to 10,000 bottles CB. **Visits:** M. Taudin,
tel.56 76 86 56. **Direct sales:** Cru d'Arrançon, Preignac,
33210 Langon. **Retail sales.**

A few years ago they were still crushing the harvest underfoot here and the *cru*
was called "Cru du Violet". But things have changed – Jean Taudin, who is a fifth-
generation Preignac grower, has mechanized his press and even thought of taking
the name of Arrançon, where the largest part of the estate is situated, as the name of
his château. His vines are between Suduiraut and Yquem, near Malle and at Fargues
in the area called Partarieux. But in the end, the Taudins decided not to haul down
the colours and the short-lived Cru d'Arrançon has once again become Violet. Jean

Taudin used to sell wine in bulk but has now adopted château bottling. His wines are traditional and conscientiously made. Since 1987, Roland Taudin, Jean's son, has run the estate, but his father's influence is still very much in evidence in the cellar.

Arrieux (Château des)

Commune: Preignac. **Proprietor:** Hubert Lacombe. Consultant oenologist: Albert Bouyx. **Size of vineyard:** 6 hectares. **Average age of vines:** 30 years. **Varieties:** 15% sauvignon, 70% sémillon, 15% muscadelle. **Production:** 15 *tonneaux*, 12,000 bottles CB. **Visits:** Wednesday and Saturday mornings. Tel. 56 63 33 54. **Direct sales and by mail order:** in France. Hubert Lacombe, Preignac, 33210 Langon. **Retail sales:** partly in bulk.

Lying between Château de Malle and Château Suduiraut, near Bastor-Lamontagne, the Arrieux vineyard is sheltered from western winds by the natural slope of the land. Its six hectares lie in one single stretch on land which is humus-bearing to a degree, composed of a mixture of sand and gravels lying on a subsoil of pure gravel. From this, the wine draws its unctuous character and is characterized by a perfume of honey which can sometimes be extremely powerful (I sometimes think I could spread this *cru* on toast for breakfast!). The muscadelle is to the fore with its sunny exoticism. At the turn of the century, harvesters volunteered in huge numbers because of the high quality of the grapes – modern wine enthusiasts should be queuing up here!

Barjuneau Chauvin (Domaine de)

Commune: Sauternes. **Proprietors:** Société Etienne et Philippe Fouquet. **Size of vineyard:** 6 hectares. **Average age of vines:** 25 years. **Varieties:** 10% sauvignon, 85% sémillon, 5% muscadelle. **Production:** 15 *tonneaux*, 10,000 bottles CB. **Visits:** possible everyday. M. Fouquet, tel. 56 63 62 57. **Direct sales and by mail order:** in France. Domaine de Barjuneau Chauvin, Sauternes, 33210 Langon. **Retail sales:** through the trade.

Situated on the south side of the commune of Sauternes, not far from the village, the vineyard lies on a south-west facing hill. Barjuneau and Chauvin are names of tiny localities on the land register and are of ancient origin. The first probably means "new meadow" in the Gascon dialect. This little estate has been in the Fouquet family since 1938. Today Etienne and Philippe together make a wine to their own satisfaction. Their clients demonstrate theirs quite regularly. The wines have won prizes at exhibitions and competitions, and they represent a fine tradition. They are sweet without being excessively so and very lively, with body which is well constituted but supple. They are already soft "en primeur" and develop nicely with time, being capable of ageing as well as any *cru classé*. The 1983 vintage is particularly to be recommended.

Bastor-Lamontagne (Château)

Commune: Preignac. **Proprietor:** Crédit Foncier de France. Director: André Hamelin. Estate manager: Jean Baup. Cellar master: Jean Bayejo. Consultant oenologist: Pierre Sudraud. **Size of vineyard:** 40 hectares. **Average age of vines:** 20 to 25 years. **Varieties:** 20% sauvignon, 70% sémillon, 10% muscadelle. **Production:** 120,000 bottles CB. **Visits:** Monday to Friday from 8.30 a.m. to 12.30 p.m. and 2 to 6 p.m. Jean Baup, estate manager, tel. 56 63 27 66. **Direct sales and by mail order:** in France and abroad. Crédit Foncier de France, 19, rue des Capucines, service des Domaines, 75050 Paris Cedex 01, or Château Bastor-Lamontagne, Preignac, 33210 Langon. **Retail sales:** approximately 50%.

"Whoever puts his money in wine makes a good investment." The Crédit Foncier de France delights in quoting Colin Muset, the troubadour from Champagne, and adds two further observations:

"The wine-lover who buys the wine of Bastor-Lamontagne makes a good investment. The Crédit Foncier de France undoubtedly made a shrewd move in buying this estate in 1936."

Then the reasoning of the banking house becomes technical: "By and large, the people of France know the Crédit Foncier well for it has enabled the majority of them to become property owners. The most recent statistics show that since 1950

Bastor-Lamontagne did not compete in the 1855 classification.

the firm in the rue des Capucines has financed more than three million mortgages, so housing more than ten million people. The granting of loans for housing is therefore the branch of activity best known to the public. On the other hand, except for a few privileged individuals, the viticultural activities of this company are not well known in France."

Before looking any further at Bastor-Lamontagne itself, I would like to ask one question of the great tycoons at the Crédit Foncier de France. Out of the three million lodgings constructed over the last forty years, how many had a wine-cellar or even just a room for storing wine?

In the face of the crisis created by the *Front populaire* (the leftist government of 1936), the Crédit Foncier de France secured the backing of the Vicomte de Larochebrochard, representing the Milleret heirs, themselves descendants of the Larrieu family. In 1850, the vineyard of Lamontagne, belonging to Amédée Larrieu, was the largest producer of wines in Preignac after Suduiraut. Charles Cocks ranked it seventh in quality. But Larrieu disdained the 1855 classification, in which he refused to compete: he was also the owner of Haut-Brion in the Graves at Pessac, and he was entirely satisfied with just one place as *Premier Cru!*

With forty hectares of vines, Château Bastor-Lamontagne remains one of the largest vine-growing estates in Sauternes. The wines have a tendency to be "pale". They are characterized by a slightly biting savour, reminiscent of certain Barsacs. A Bastor-Lamontagne in a great year will always be better than a *cru classé* in a mediocre year.

Baylieu (Domaine)

Commune: Fargues. **Proprietor:** Denis Sarraute. Consultant oenologist: Jean-Paul Pauquet. **Size of vineyard:** 6 hectares. **Average age of vines:** 40 years. **Varieties:** 20% sauvignon, 70% sémillon, 10% muscadelle. **Production:** 16 *tonneaux*, 10,000 bottles CB. **Direct sales:** Denis Sarraute, Fargues, 33210 Langon. Tel. 56 63 50 89. **Retail sales.** *An enterprise which is both small-scale and commercial in the best sense of the terms, producing wine of an honest average quality.*

Bêchereau (Château)

Commune: Bommes. **Proprietor:** Franck Deloubes. Consultant oenologist: Jean-Paul Pauquet. **Size of vineyard:** 10 hectares. **Average age of vines:** 25 years. **Varieties:** 15% sauvignon, 80% sémillon, 5% muscadelle. **Production:** 25,000 bottles CB. **Visits:** Daily from 8 a.m. to noon and 2 to 7 p.m. Tel. 56 63 61 73. **Direct sales and by mail order:** in France and abroad. M. Deloubes, Château Bêchereau, Bommes, 33210 Langon. *Underground cellars (the only ones in Sauternes) hold mature wines which can reach semi-classic quality.*

Béquet (Château) 🍷 → Rabaud-Promis

Bouyot (Château)

Commune: Barsac. **Proprietor:** Madame Geneviève Jammy-Fonbeney. Consultant oenologist: Pierre Sudraud. **Size of vineyard:** 13.5 hectares. **Average age of vines:** 30 years. **Varieties:** 3% sauvignon, 95% sémillon, 2% muscadelle. **Production:** 37 *tonneaux*, 15,000 bottles CB. **Visits:** everyday from 9 a.m. to 7 p.m. Weekends by appointment only. Tel. 56 27 19 46. **Direct sales and by mail order:** in France. Madame Geneviève Jammy-Fonbeney, Le Bouyot, Barsac, 33720 Podensac. **Retail sales:** sales can be made either to merchants direct or through a broker and in the same way the wine is distributed either in bulk or in bottle.

When Geneviève Jammy-Fonbeney takes it into her head to tour her estate, she starts at the small plot of vines in front of her house. Then she makes for a large patch of vines –five hectares – between Ménota and Myrat. And, if she really wants to leave no stone unturned, her visit will take her to a plot adjoining Coutet and another at la Pinesse. A wide variety of different types of land therefore combine to make the wine of Bouyot. Today the proprietor's son, Bertrand is in charge of both cellars and vines. He is the fourth generation to work the estate. Whereas his predecessors were content to sell in bulk to the trade in Bordeaux, from the 1985 vintage Bertrand has carried out his intention of "increasing bottling". The quality of his wine entirely merits this decision. However, it would be desirable if this policy could be supported by more dynamic marketing strategies, especially abroad where the label remains relatively little known. In my opinion this wine represents among the best value for money to be found in the Barsac appellation. It has a fine, rather deep colour. Its bouquet is founded on an alcoholic base. In the mouth, it is powerful, surprisingly so for a Barsac, with a pleasant flavour of cooked plum.

Brassens-Guiteronde (Ch.) → Guiteronde du Hayot

Briatte (Château)

Commune: Preignac. **Proprietors:** Messrs Roudès Père & Fils. **Size of vineyard:** 9 hectares. **Average age of vines:** 35 years. **Varieties:** 5% sauvignon, 90% sémillon, 5% muscadelle. **Production:** 25 *tonneaux*, 14,000 bottles CB. **Visits:** tel. 56 63 00 54. **Direct sales and by mail order:** in France. Messrs Roudès Père & Fils, Château Briatte, Preignac, 33210 Langon.

The result of merging several plots into one unit, Château Briatte was unknown in the ranks of Sauternes wines at the beginning of the century. The 9 hectares of vines are close to Châteaux d'Yquem, Suduiraut and Lafaurie-Peyraguey, a distinguished neighbourhood if ever there was one. The *cru* of Briatte was confirmed in November 1942 by the regional commission controlling all the wines with an *appellation contrôlée* in the Gironde. At the time, it was customary for the ceiling price to be fixed administratively for each category of wines. For the 1941 vintage, the sale price of the wines of Briatte, was strictly forbidden to exceed 60,000 francs per *tonneau.* Today, by mutual agreement, you can negotiate the price of Briatte wine directly and you have the right to fix the ceiling price yourself. Don't worry too much however: should it be Roudès Père et Fils who announced their minimum price to you, it would still remain reasonable.

Broustet (Château)

2e cru classé

Commune: Barsac. **Proprietor:** S.E.V. Fournier. Cultivation supervisor: R. Faugère. Cellar master: M. Cazenave. Consultant oenologist: Pierre Sudraud. **Size of vineyard:** 16 hectares. **Average age of vines:** 40 years. **Varieties:** 25% sauvignon, 63% sémillon, 12% muscadelle. **Production:** 36,000 bottles CB. **Visits:** M. Faugère, tel. 56 27 16 27. **Direct sales and by mail order:** in France. S.E.V. Fournier, B.P. 28, 33330 Saint-Emilion. **Retail sales:** through Bordeaux.

The great-grandfather of the current proprietors established the largest cooperage in the *département* at Broustet. It was he who, at the end of the last century, accepted the request of Bordeaux's chamber of commerce to establish official standards for the *barrique bordelaise,* as follows:

The *barrique bordelaise* is made of wood from the heart of the oak's trunk, which must be cut while still green, splitting it along the grain. It holds 225 litres with a tolerance of plus or minus 2 litres. It is 91 centimetres long. At its widest point (the bilge or *bouge*) the external circumference is 2.18 metres. It is principally used for ageing wine in the cellars, for it is not constructed with a view to being transported. It is made up of seventeen staves (or *douelles*) which are 16 to 18 millimetres thick

Generally speaking, the great crus keep the traditional wooden case.

at either end and 12 to 14 millimetres thick at the bilge. Metal bands (hoop-irons or *feuillards*) have replaced hoop-wood of chestnut, which makes rolling and general handling of the casks easier. The hole on the bilge is called the bunghole (or *bonde*). The hole at the end (correctly called the head) of the cask is the drain (or *esquive*). The volume can be determined in three different ways:

– by decanting, or *dépotage,* which gives the exact quantity of liquid drawn from a *barrique*;

– by weighing, or *pesage,* which gives the difference in the *barrique's* weight when empty and when full;

– by gauging, or *veltage,* that is in measuring the inside of a *barrique* by means of a specially graduated ruler called a *velte.*

The regions of France which produce the best oak are the Limousin, the Bourbonnais (especially in the Allier *département)* and Alsace.

Today it is Eric Fournier who runs this family estate, as he does also the famous Château Canon in Saint-Emilion. He has had the unusual idea of treating his muscadelle vines against botrytis to prevent them from rotting. The wine of Château Broustet is distinguished, elegant and not too sweet. It is best appreciated in its early youth when its primary aromas are still intact, giving a bouquet which is essentially floral.

Caillou (Château)

2e cru classé

Commune: Barsac. **Proprietor:** Madame Joseph Bravo. Directors: Madame Pierre and Monsieur Bravo. Consultant oenologists: M. Llorca and M. Peynaud. **Size of vineyard:** 15 hectares. **Average age of vines:** 22 years. **Varieties:** 10% sauvignon, 90% sémillon. **Production:** 30 to 50,000 bottles CB. **Visits:** by appointment. M. Bravo, tel. 56 27 16 38 or Madame Pierre, tel. 56 27 22 59. **Direct sales and by mail order:** in France. Madame Joseph Bravo, Château Caillou, Barsac, 33720 Podensac. **Retail sales**.

Caillou's label has not changed for a century, except for the names of the proprietor and the previous appellation "Haut-Barsac" which, being no longer officially recognized as an AOC, is now not legally valid. The vineyard's entry in the land register too, has not been modified since the historical classification of 1855. Its 15 hectares are to the south-west of the commune near the hamlet of Mathalin, not far from Châteaux Myrat and Climens. The residence, a gracious manor-house with two bell-turrets, emerges from its vines like a rocky island from the sea. This excellent and ancient 2ᵉ *cru classé* belonged to the Sarraute family throughout the nineteenth century. In 1909, Château Caillou was bought at auction by Joseph

Monsieur Bravo.

Ballan, Madame Bravo's grandfather. According to today's proprietors, every year Caillou's wine has perfumes of the most subtly varied fruits: dried apricot and peach flesh in 1983; fresh fruits with mint and wild thyme in 1982; apple, hazel nut and almond in 1981; currants (and rum!) in 1978. The traditional practice of maintaining separate *cuvées* known as "crème de tête" has never been abandoned here and Château Caillou proudly bottles a "private cuvée" in the good years (rather in the style of Krug champagne). I would be ready to swear that the distinctive aroma of the "private cuvée" of 1983 is unmistakable – passion fruit.

Cameron (Château)

Commune: Bommes. **Proprietor:** Paul Lanneluc. **Tenant:** Pierre Guinabert. Consultant oenologist: Pierre Sudraud. **Size of vineyard:** 8.43 hectares. **Average age of vines:** 30 years. **Varieties:** 100% sémillon. **Production:** 20,000 bottles CB. **Visits:** everyday, preferably by appointment. Pierre Guinabert, tel. 56 27 16 39. **Direct sales and by mail order:** in France and abroad. Monsieur Pierre Guinabert, Haut-Bommes, Bommes, 33210 Langon. **Retail sales:** through the trade.

Pierre Guinabert has run this estate as a tenant since 1981. He runs his vineyard in traditional craftsman fashion and yields are maintained at a relatively low level. He declares that he is still very much in love with "the best white wines in the world". His wines are rich and rather dark in colour, impressively powerful, and have aromas of vanilla sometimes bordering on oxidation. Their solid structure is confirmed by firm balancing in their acidity, in which there can be detected a hint of volatile vapours. It is truly wine produced in the old-fashioned way which will suit conservative wine lovers perfectly. Rent for the tenancy is paid in kind. Its equivalent in wine, selected by Paul Lanneluc, is then marketed under the name of Domaine Raymond Louis, which cannot, strictly speaking, be considered as a secondary label of Château Cameron.

Camperos (Château) ⚲ → Pebayle

Cantegril (Château) ⚲ → Doisy Daëne

Caplane (Domaine de)

Commune: Sauternes. **Proprietors:** J. Trijasson and A. Dubernet. **Size of vineyard:** 17 hectares. **Average age of vines:** 40 years. **Varieties:** 10% sauvignon, 80% sémillon, 10% muscadelle. **Production:** 18 to 20,000 bottles CB. **Direct sales and by mail order:** in France. J. Trijasson, Domaine de Caplane, Sauternes, 33210 Langon. Tel. 56 63 62 11. **Retail sales:** 50% in the *barrique*, 50% in bottle.

The Dubernet-Trijasson family has taken 30 years to unite a number of fragmented parcels, adding occasional purchases to them. Today Caplane's vineyard is of an impressive size, 17 hectares, situated mainly between Yquem on the north and Château d'Arche on the south. Its terrain is of excellent quality, the wines are very traditional in style. Once the label mentioned the vineyard's proximity to Château Yquem and claimed the Haut-Sauternes appellation. This alluring label disappeared some years ago but the genuine progress in quality which has been achieved meanwhile can readily be perceived.

Jean Trijasson.

Carbonnieu (Domaine de)

Commune: Bommes. **Proprietors:** Marc and Alain Charrier. **Size of vineyard:** 10 hectares. **Average age of vines:** 25 years. **Varieties:** 5% sauvignon, 90% sémillon, 5% muscadelle. **Production:** 30 *tonneaux*, 12,000 bottles CB. **Direct sales and by mail order:** Marc and Alain Charrier, Les Chons, Bommes, 33210 Langon. Tel. 56 63 60 78. **Retail sales:** two thirds of the production is sold in bulk for export. *Family tradition has been transmitted from father to son. The estate produces wines of average standard.*

Carles (Château de)

Commune: Barsac. **Proprietor:** G.F.A. du Château de Carles. Director: Michel Pascaud. Consultant oenologist: C.E.I.OE. in Cadillac. **Size of vineyard:** 9.08 hectares. **Average age of vines:** 25 to 30 years. **Varieties:** 10% sauvignon, 90% sémillon. **Production:** 25 *tonneaux*, 22,000 bottles CB. **Sales by mail order:** in France and abroad. Château de Carles, Barsac, 33720 Podensac. Tel. 56 27 07 19. **Retail sales:** château-bottled production exclusively through the merchants and specialist shops.

Coutet, Climens, Caillou and Myrat form a golden rectangle marking the limits of the high plateau of Barsac. The plots producing the wine of Carles are to be found within this perimeter, and are typical of the Barsac appellation. The predominance of sémillon gives a delicate savour and Michel Pascaud, the present tenant of the estate, is quite right not to wish to change the proportions. He is a qualified agriculturalist and maintains a long family tradition which goes way back to 1859. By nature he is reserved, careful and a perfectionist. His aim is to produce the highest quality, certain that he will always find a taker.

The history of Carles began in the fifteenth century. It knew moments of glory in the eighteenth century and dark days during the Revolution. At the time of the 1855 classification, the estate belonged to a Dutch wine merchant who had no difficulty in selling the whole of his production to the Netherlands. He failed to participate in the competition for the classification, considering it a fleeting French whim. Carles has none the less since been recognized as one of the *crus* which most deserve to be reclassified. The wine too merits discovery. It has all the distinction of a high-class Barsac. I can recommend it to the wine lovers for the nobility of its birth and its sincerity.

Chante l'Oiseau (Château)　　Ⓨ Ⓨ Ⓨ Ⓨ Ⓨ

Commune: Barsac. **Proprietor:** Philippe Meynard. Consultant oenologist: Jean-Paul Pauquet. **Size of vineyard:** 3.5 hectares. **Average age of vines:** 30 years. **Varieties:** 40% sauvignon, 50% sémillon, 10% muscadelle. **Production:** 11 *tonneaux*, 5,000 bottles CB. **Direct sales and by mail order:** in France. M. Meynard, La Pinesse, Barsac, 33720 Podensac. Tel. 56 27 19 66. **Retail sales:** by the *tonneaux*.

Philippe Meynard became the lord of Chante l'Oiseau in 1964 "for the love of nature". His *cru* is situated on the plateau of la Pinesse towards the south-east of the appellation. He runs the estate on organic principles, preferring to dispense with chemical products and treatments. His yields are quite high and the main part of his production is sold to the négociant trade in bulk.

Climens (Château)　　Ⓨ Ⓨ Ⓨ Ⓨ Ⓨ

ler cru classé

Commune: Barsac. **Proprietor:** Lucien Lurton. Director: Maurice Garros. Estate manager: Madame André Janin. Vineyard manager and cellar master: Christian Broustaut. Consultant oenologist: Emile Peynaud. **Size of vineyard:** 29 hectares. **Average age of vines:** 50 years. **Varieties:** 2% sauvignon, 98% sémillon. **Production:** 54,000 bottles CB. **Visits:** Vignobles Lurton, tel. 56 88 70 20. **Direct sales:** Château Climens, Barsac, 33720 Podensac. **Retail sales:** through Bordeaux.

In the fifteenth century, a certain Jehan Climens (or Climenz), collected the landing tax from boats on the Garonne, giving the ship's master, as a "certificate of origin", a branch of cypress, a practice called "cypressat". But was Climens first and foremost a family name or a place name? No one knows. At the time of the 1855 classification, it belonged to the Lacoste family. The Gounouilhou family succeeded them and, during the first half of this century, Climens maintained a position among the first ranks of the wines of Barsac. After this, an inheritance occasioned a joint ownership and there followed a period of neglect. During the sixties, the property was put up 　97

Château Climens is pure gold – almost white gold.

for sale and found no takers. And yet, what land and what potential quality the
cru had! It so happened that I started to take a close interest in Château Climens
in 1970. I particularly remember taking François Rochas there (son of the beautiful
Hélène), who came very near to buying it but was put off by the huge amount of
work to be done on the neglected vineyard and in the badly equipped cellar. A
saviour arrived in the shape of Lucien Lurton. He snapped it up immediately for
a (modest) handful of some million centimes. In accordance with his viticultural
philosophy, he restored the vineyard by rationalizing the estate. As regards wine-

making, he took out an all-risk insurance policy when he asked Professor Emile Peynaud to supervise vinification. The results are extremely successful. But (dare I say it) Climens could doubtless do even better. When the sale of Climens to Lurton was clinched, one of the Gounouilhou heirs, Philippe Lassus, was kind enough to present me with a collection of old bottles of rare old vintages. This was by way of thanking me for my intervention. Since then, I have been able to study Climens's riches closely. It is a fantastic *cru*! I have never tasted such wine, incomparable for its delicacy, its subtle harmony, and its delicious vivacity. At the risk of offending one of my very good friends who swears only by Yquem, I would say that I have often preferred the "Prince of Barsac" to the "King of Sauternes". So here is my advice: if you come across an auction catalogue featuring a Climens dating from the beginning of the century, buy it with utter confidence; you will not be disappointed.

But to return to the present and to more recent vintages: Climens always has a rare finesse, but it has become rather "modern". That is all well and good for a *cru* of lesser breeding. In my opinion, Climens should incarnate the very quintessence of Barsac. Otherwise what else would stand in its place? However, for Brigitte Lurton-Belondrade, daughter of Lucien Lurton (who furthermore owns Château Brane-Cantenac, Durfort-Vivens), this jewel in the family crown holds a very special place in her affections. Climens is well on its way to re-establishing its majestic stature.

Clos Haut-Peyraguey (Château)

1er cru classé

Commune: Bommes. **Proprietor:** G.F.A. du Clos Haut-Peyraguey. Director and cellar master: Jacques Pauly Consultant oenologist: Pierre Sudraud. **Size of vineyard:** 15 hectares. **Average age of vines:** 30 years. **Varieties:** 15% sauvignon, 83% sémillon, 2% muscadelle. **Production:** 40,000 bottles CB. **Visits:** everyday; groups are requested to make a prior appointment. Monsieur Pauly, tel. 56 63 61 53. **Direct sales and by mail order:** in France. GFA du Clos Haut-Peyraguey, Bommes, 33210 Langon. **Retail sales:** Dourthe Frères and Kressmann, 35 rue de Bordeaux, 33290 Parempuyre.

At their highest point, the vineyards of Bommes reach an altitude of 72 metres. The boundary of the commune is in the little valley which separates Bommes from Sauternes. Haut-Peyraguey is situated just opposite Yquem on the other slope and at the same height. The *cru*'s history was confused with that of Château Peyraguey until 1879, when the two proprietors, Farinel and Grédy, sold the highest part of the estate to a Parisian chemist called Grillon. From then on it was called "Clos Haut-Peyraguey", without losing its right to the title of *Premier Cru Classé*. Eugène Garbay and Fernand Ginestet bought it in 1914. Seven years later, the former gave his share to his grandsons, Pierre and Bernard Pauly. In 1937, Fernand Ginestet handed over his share to the family firm of the Garbay heirs. Since 1969, Jacques Pauly has run the estate. The vineyards have been restored strictly according to the rules of the art, after having suffered a certain degree of neglect. The present choice and proportions of varieties seem to me to be absolutely ideal.

The wines of Clos Haut-Peyraguey are typically modern in style. They are rich in aromas springing more from finesse than from concentration. Hubrecht Duijker uses the word "slenderness" to describe them, which seems to be a judicious term. To be more precise, this qualification should be accompanied by ideas of lightness and delicacy. It is true that Jacques Pauly could be accused (and some people

99

This great classic has moved with the times.

have not hesitated to do so) with developing his *cru* towards what Professor Emile Peynaud calls "pale Sauternes" even though he has at his disposition all the essential elements (soil, subsoil, microclimate, etc.) to make a very great classic wine. But he is not entirely to be blamed since the wine he produces is contemporary and is what the consumer wants. Opinions differ. I sit on the fence. But I do reproach Jacques Pauly with one thing, namely with recommending the use of his wine "creatively" for cooking.

Closiot (Château)

Commune: Barsac. **Proprietor:** Hector Soizeau. Director and manager: Françoise Soizeau. Consultant oenologist: Albert Bouyx. **Size of vineyard:** 8 hectares. **Average age of vines:** 25 years. **Varieties:** 3% sauvignon, 95% sémillon, 2% muscadelle. **Production:** 25 *tonneaux*, 7,000 bottles CB. **Visits:** by appointment only. Mademoiselle Françoise Soizeau, tel. 56 27 05 92. **Direct sales:** Château Closiot, Boîte postale 17, Barsac, 33720 Podensac. **Retail sales:** through the trade.

Alban Duprat, Hector Soizeau's father-in-law, bought this little estate in 1934. On Closiot's tower there are crosses, a reminder that the site must have been a stopping-off point for pilgrins on their way to Santiago de Compostella. Hector Soizeau and his wife cultivate their vineyard with devoted care. It is essentially planted with sémillon. But they also carefully retain discreet proportions of sauvignon and muscadelle to give their wine a hint of originality, rather like a beauty spot on the neck of some classical beauty. Their daughter Françoise is also involved in the family's work and shares her parent's passion. The visitor will always be welcomed with genuine cordiality, and so he will have time to discover wines of stirring authenticity: supple, round, rich and full-bodied.

Comet-Magey (Château)

Commune: Preignac. **Proprietors:** Pierre and Yvette Barbe.
Consultant oenologist: Jean-Paul Pauquet. **Size of vineyard:** 6 hectares. **Average age of vines:** 30 years. **Varieties:** 10% sauvignon, 85% sémillon, 5% muscadelle. **Production:** 16 *tonneaux*, 9,000 bottles C.B. **Visits:** tel. 56 63 02 39, individual customers only. **Direct sales and by mail order:** Monsieur Pierre Barbe, lieu-dit Boutoc, Preignac, 33210 Langon. **Retail sales.**

Among other family papers, Pierre Barbe has an original document drawn up in 1726 by the court notary in Barsac. It is an *acte de baillette* (or lease), for several arpents (acres) of land, granted by the local lord, Laurent de Sauvage d'Iquem, to a worker from Preignac by the name of Pierre La Saubatjue du Magé. To ensure that his estate was going to be worked properly, the lord of the noble house of Yquem surrounded himself with a wealth of precautions. It is specified that the lessee is "pledged feudally", which for the time seems somewhat anachronistic. The agreement includes a clause binding the lessee to pay an annual rent plus a quarter of everything produced on the estate, whether in cereal crops or in grapes. The worker did not have the right to sublet or to subcontract the work to a third party. But the harvests were to be supervised by the lord's henchmen. If the crops were insufficient, the lease was forfeit and the lessee could expect to be condemned to a fine, even if the deficiency were due to illness. As for the wine, the lord provided "four vessels of equal size placed in the most practical place for the custodian". The custodian had to watch over the harvest and the lease stipulates that he was to be fed by the lessee, each eating the same fare. Moreover, the lord chose the wine from the vat which seemed the best. The same was true for the corn, "collected and piled in sheaves in the presence of the said custodian who will choose whatever he wishes to make up the said lord's quota".

Working for the lord of Yquem was certainly no holiday. But the clause which pleases me most is the one which speaks of "the direct annual and perpetual land rent: a pair of roasting chickens, brought and delivered by the said tenant to the said lord in his noble house of Yquem every year each Christmas Day without fail". And I can recall as in a dream the late Marquis Bertrand de Lur Saluces declaring with what I might describe as atavistic conviction: "And you know my dear fellow, Yquem is delicious with roast chicken!" And so is Comet-Magey, the republican wine of Pierre Barbe.

Couite (Domaine de)

Commune: Preignac. **Proprietor:** Claude Deloubes. Consultant oenologist: Jean-Paul Pauquet. **Size of vineyard:** 1.6 hectares. **Average age of vines:** 40 years. **Varieties:** 33% sauvignon, 33% sémillon, 33% muscadelle. **Production:** 4 *tonneaux*, 2,000 bottles CB. **Direct sales and by mail order:** in France. Claude Deloubes, Domaine de Couite, Preignac, 33210 Langon. Tel. 56 63 22 03. **Retail sales:** every other year unsold wine goes to the trade.

"About every two years, I offer whatever wine has not been sold in bottle to a broker who sells it to a merchant." Claude Deloubes does not run after clients. If they arrive, so much the better (for them). His father bought the estate in 1930. You ask about the Couite 1937? A wine of absolute splendour, which spoiled the gourmets for a long time. The '47 too was very good but not up to the '37. The '53, however, was as good as the '37. As for the '75, it is beginning to equal the '53." After this awards list, Claude Deloubes makes no further pronouncement. We shall see. Perhaps the '85 will be as good as the '37, but it is far too early to tell.

Coutet (Château)

1er cru classé

Commune: Barsac. **Proprietor:** Société civile du Château Coutet. Director: Marcel Baly. Vineyard manager: Eric Tasson. Cellar master: Claude Pascaud. Consultant oenologist: CEIOE. in Cadillac. **Size of vineyard:** 36 hectares. **Average age of vines:** 40 years. **Varieties:** 23% sauvignon, 75% sémillon, 2% muscadelle. **Production:** 90,000 bottles CB. **Visits:** Sylvie Pascaud, tel. 56 27 15 46. **Direct sales and by mail order:** in France. Château Coutet S.C., Barsac, 33720 Podensac. **Retail sales:** Alexis Lichine & Cie, 109, rue Achard, 33028 Bordeaux Cedex.

Placed at the head of the wines of Barsac in the 1855 classification, Château Coutet can claim a prestigious history. To start with it was a military encampment during the Hundred Years War. At that time, the vineyards of Barsac were barely developed. The wines produced were drunk on the spot, principally by local clerics and soldiers. For more than a century, from 1810 to 1922, it was in the hands of the wealthy Lur Saluces family (who also owned Yquem, Filhot, Malle, Fargues and other equally productive though less celebrated vineyards). It then passed into the

Château Coutet's architecture has kept its original military air.

hands of a manufacturer of hydraulic presses based in Lyons. This Monsieur Guy had two daughters, of whom one, Madame Thomas, was widowed while still young. Her children's private tutor, the priest Rolland, devoted himself body and soul to the household, so much so that he forsook the cloth in favour of the vine and married the widow and her fine estate. Edmond Rolland became a remarkable grower. In love with his work, he maintained Coutet's very high level of quality. He also became the vice-chancellor of Bordeaux's wine academy. Nevertheless I believe his former vocation must sometimes have preyed on his conscience. I remember an astonishing scene – Rolland, one-time ordained priest, drinking a baptismal toast in Bordeaux wine to the first edition of the review *Vin, table et tourisme*, in the great hall of the CIVB I was young and quite astounded. It was a solemn act. The celebrant appeared serene, but his hand trembled and several drops fell on his shoe.

In 1977, after the death of Madame Rolland, the estate was sold to Marcel Baly, an industrialist from Strasbourg, and a great epicurean, aesthete and gourmet. He took every care to keep Coutet in the first ranks of the wines of Barsac. For some

years, this *cru* has been distributed exclusively by the firm of Alexis Lichine and Co. Its principal characteristic is its aromatic richness combined with great stamina. In style, it has tended to become "pale", but in the good years, just as in the time of Madame Rolland, Marcel Baly continues to produce a small quantity of prestige wine, labelled "Cuvée Madame".

Coy (Domaine du)

Commune: Sauternes. **Proprietor:** Roger Biarnès. Consultant oenologist: Monsieur Bouyx and CEIOE in Cadillac. **Size of vineyard:** 7 hectares. **Average age of vines:** 20 to 35 years. **Varieties:** 15% sauvignon, 80% sémillon, 5% muscadelle. **Production:** 15,000 bottles CB. **Visits:** weekdays only. Monsieur and Madame Biarnès, tel. 56 27 20 27. **Direct sales and by mail order:** in France and abroad. Roger Biarnès, Château de Navarro, 33720 Illats. **Retail sales:** through the trade.

The small vineyard of Coy is to be found in the little place name called "Le Pajot", between Yquem and Guiraud. It is one of the possessions of the Biarnès family, who are also proprietors of Château Suau (see below) in Barsac. The estate was bought a good forty years ago from Monsieur Lanneluc by Roger Biarnès' father. The wines of Domaine du Coy are distinguished by their elegance and lightness. They have a "modern" tendency, are pale straw yellow in colour and are very limpid. Lively to the nose, supple on the palate, they will never numb the taste-buds and should preferably be drunk while young. They are "good little Sauternes", honest and thirst-quenching.

Doisy Daëne (Château)

2e cru classé

Commune: Barsac. **Proprietor:** Pierre Dubourdieu. Consultant oenologist: Denis Dubourdieu. **Size of vineyard:** 14 hectares. **Average age of vines:** 35 years. **Varieties:** 15% sauvignon, 75% sémillon, 10% muscadelle. **Production:** 40,000 bottles CB. **Visits:** Pierre Dubourdieu, tel. 56 27 15 84. **Direct sales and by mail order:** in France. Château Doisy Daëne, Barsac, 33720 Podensac. **Retail sales:** through Bordeaux and for export.

Daëne, also written "Daine" or "Daenne" in the nineteenth century, is the name of a family which owned Doisy for a good number of years. The status of the *cru* between 1855 and 1875 is confusing, but can be summarized as follows:

1850: Charles Cocks cites the *crus* of Barsac. The best three are Coutet, Climenz, Daëne. No mention of Doisy.

1855: The official classification: Doisy, belonging to "Deane", is cited second among the *deuxièmes crus* of Barsac and Sauternes.

1864: William Frank ranks "Daenne" twenty-fourth among the wines of Barsac, whereas the estate of the widow Debans-Ellien is fourth.

1868: Charles Cocks gives Doisy (Daenne) seventh place among the best wines of Barsac. The same year, William Frank mentions the *deuxième cru* of Doisy, belonging to Monsieur Debans Saint-Cyr, which he places in fourth position.

1871: Frank continues the classification.

1874: Edouard Féret confirms Charles Cocks's classification. Doisy "Daine" is in seventh position after Doisy-Védrines and Doisy-Gravas. This sequence illustrates both the ups and downs of the history of Bordeaux viticulture (at a time when the

Doisy Daëne is a fine example of an excellent and well-ordered Sauternes estate.

idea of *cru* had yet to be defined) and the rivalries of the growers who, after the *Classement*, were already trying to outdo one another.

To step quickly into more modern times, we find Georges Dubourdieu, who bought Doisy Daëne in 1924, and his son, Pierre, who succeeded him in 1945. He has an inquisitive nature, respecting traditional methods as much as he enjoys experimenting. Helped by his son, Denis Dubourdieu, professor at the Institut d'Oenologie de Bordeaux, he dreams of a Barsac untreated with sulphur. Constantly balancing past, present and future, he produces wines of outstanding quality.

Here are some notes on recent vintages:

1976: A rather deep, old gold colour. Nose of mirabelle plum, apricot, crystallized orange, white peach. Gracious and of youthful distinction. Very classic.

1981: Straw yellow in colour, slighly woody nose, smoky vapours, aromas of acacia, crusty bread, gingerbread, together with hints of balsam. Powerful and harmonious.

1982: A fine golden yellow with aromas of orange zest, mint, and smoky vapours. Flattering and of great charm. It will develop well.

1983: Golden yellow. An ever-unfolding bouquet: sage, mirabelle plum, undergrowth, peach, vanilla, acacia; ample, very full-bodied without being heavy. A wine with a tremendous future, whose power needs ageing to be appreciated.

1985: Little botrytis, but dried up grapes, harvested in the sun and dessicated by the frost. Concentrated, long finish with almond aromas. Should develop very well.

1986: Depth and elegance. Enchanting roasted aromas. A very great wine.

1988: A very round and delicate structure, very well balanced, powerful. A great vintage full of elegance and finesse.

1989: Appears to predict a very great vintage, close in style to 1943.

Doisy Dubroca (Château)

2e cru classé

Commune: Barsac. **Proprietor:** Monsieur Lucien Lurton. Tel. 56 27 15 33. **Size of vineyard:** 4.5 hectares. **Average age of vines:** 25 years. **Varieties:** 10% sauvignon, 90% sémillon. **Production:** 5,100 bottles CB. **Retail sales:** through the Bordeaux trade.

When he bought Climens in 1971, Lucien Lurton also acquired Doisy Dubroca. These *crus* have been linked together since 1880, at the time of the marriage of a Dubroca daughter to a Gounouilhou, the proprietor-to-be of Climens. The two estates are run in identical fashion. Doisy Dubroca, by its size and stature, is truly Climens's younger brother.

Doisy-Védrines (Château)

2e cru classé

Commune: Barsac. **Proprietor:** Pierre Castéja. Vineyard manager: Lionel Me. Consultant oenologist: Monsieur Llorca. **Size of vineyard:** 20 hectares. **Average age of vines:** 30 years. **Varieties:** 20% sauvignon, 80% sémillon. **Production:** 45 *tonneaux*, 30,000 bottles CB. **Visits:** by appointment only. Tel. 56 27 15 13. **Retail sales:** through Maison Joanne, Boîte postale 9, Fargues Saint-Hilaire, 33370 Tresses.

The house at Doisy-Védrines is a pleasant country residence.

The Chevaliers de Védrines were once the owners of this estate, to which they gave their name. They sold it in 1846 when the ancestors of the present owners became its proprietors. The line of transmission could therefore hardly be simpler. At Doisy-Védrines there is a pane of glass on which one of the Védrines wives signed her name with a diamond. The signature seems to date from 1830 but no one knows the circumstances under which it was written. However, this gives me the opportunity to suggest that the etymology of *Védrines* is "verrerie" (glass-works) or "vitrerie" (glaziery). A whole host of names derives from it.

In Louisiana, in the United States, there is a Vidrine family, founded by Jean Baptiste Lapaise Védrines, a midshipman who emigrated in 1739 at the age of twenty-seven. Jacqueline Olivier Vidrine, the present descendant of this branch "imported from France" has undertaken considerable research concerning her ancestors. After some twenty-five years of compilation, correspondence and other historical research, she mapped out the saga of the Védrines in a book she published in 1981. It is a work of great erudition.

In it, we read in particular that on May 29, 1704, a marriage took place in Barsac between Jean Védrines and Marie Raymond. The name of "Doisy-Védrines" certainly goes back to this date, for today's château was the summer residence of the Raymonds, a respected family of Bordeaux jurists. On his side, Jean Védrines, the father of the young bridegroom, was a lawyer in Sainte-Livrade near Agen. The two families undoubtedly met in the context of the legal fraternity. According to the legal documents, two vignerons on the property were witnesses to the marriage: Jean Reau and Jean Pascale. We therefore know that a vineyard existed here at the beginning of the eighteenth century. Maintained in the classical tradition, Doisy-Védrines has a place apart in the anthology of the great *crus* of Barsac. Each harvest is matured quite separately for a year in the *barriques* in which fermentation took place. The wine in each *barrique* is then tested to see whether it is worthy to be part of the "Grand Vin". Sometimes the entire harvest is declassified as Sauternes (as was the case in 1963, 1964, 1965, 1968 and 1974). I agree with Hugh Johnson when he says, "Its quality always gave me to think that it was a *Premier Cru* rather than a second." At blind tastings over the last ten years, Doisy-Védrines has distinguished itself among the firsts on several occasions. Without any possible doubt, it is one of the best wines of Barsac today. The 1988 vintage is absolutely sensational. The great art of Pierre Castéja has reached its apogee. It is almost impossible to imagine how anyone could surpass it.

Duc de Sauternes

Commune: Sauternes. **Proprietor:** Association Loi de 1901 (Maison du Sauternes). Director: Madame Lamothe. **Size of vineyard:** one per cent of the harvest of the forty-three members. **Varieties:** traditional, with 5% muscadelle. **Production:** 10,000 bottles CB. **Visits:** Madame Tracou, tel. 56 63 60 37. **Direct sales and by mail order:** in France. Maison du Sauternes, place de la Mairie, Sauternes, 33210 Langon.

This duke is in fact a child of the people which resembles in spirit to another *cave coopérative*, Marquis de Saint-Estèphe to be precise. In 1973 the Viticultural Federation of Sauternes created an association (under the law of 1901) to promote the appellation. Forty-three producers are members. Each one pays an annual subscription in wine, at the rate of 1% of his harvest. All the wine resulting from this is blended and bottled under the name Duc de Sauternes. It can be tasted and bought at the Maison du Sauternes. Naturally, it is the very synthesis of Sauternes wines and its proletarian origins in no way detract from its fine constitution and harmony: forty voices of average quality can make up an excellent choir. But each member can sing his own song, that is, display his personal production and offer it to potential customers at reasonable prices. So, at the Maison du Sauternes, we find viticulturalists with golden voices.

Dudon (Château)

Commune: Barsac. **Proprietor:** Madame J. Herteman. Director: J. Saumade-Herteman. Cellar master: M. Marquille. Consultant oenologist: C.E.I.OE. in Cadillac. **Size of vineyard:** 9 hectares. **Average age of vines:** 10 to 15 years. **Varieties:** 10% sauvignon, 90% sémillon. **Production:** 25 *tonneaux*. **Visits:** by appointment. M. Marquille, tel. 56 27 23 38. **Direct sales:** Château Dudon, Barsac, 33720 Podensac. **Retail sales:** through Bordeaux.

This Dudon should not be confused with the other Château Dudon, which is to be found in Baurech, in the appellation of Premières Côtes de Bordeaux. Château Dudon is an attractive little country house flanked by two towers, one round and one square, on each wing. It was originally built by a Comte de Dudon towards the end of the eighteenth century, and remodelled by the Pichard family in the second half of the nineteenth. It then passed into the hands of the Gaussem-Balayés of whom 107

Madame J. Herteman is the direct heiress. Situated between Coutet and Broustet, the vineyard consists of three plots surrounding the château and its grounds. It is completely walled round in accordance with the best Barsac tradition. Jacqueline Herteman, mother of three children and grandmother of five grandchildren, is closely attached to the land of Dudon. But she also has vines in Corbières and on the slopes of the Languedoc.

Traditionally distributed by the Bordeaux trade, Château Dudon is also vinified traditionally. The vineyard is in full production and gives substantial yields. But cultivation is carried out impeccably. No herbicides are used: the vines are carefully de-leafed by hand. The cellar master, M. Marquille, first practised his art at Château Coutet. He has a wealth of skill at his fingertips.

Duperneau (Domaine)

Commune: Bommes. **Proprietor:** Hector Lassauvageux. **Size of vineyard:** 3.5 hectares. **Average age of vines:** 50 years. **Varieties:** 20% sauvignon, 60% sémillon, 20% muscadelle. **Production:** 10 tonneaux. **Direct sales, mail order and retail sales:** through Château La Tour Blanche, Bommes, 33210 Langon. Tel. 56 63 61 55. Hector Lassauvageux held the fort till he had counted over eighty years of harvests, but his *cru* has now been taken on lease by Château La Tour Blanche at Bommes. (q.v.).

Fargues (Château de)

Commune: Fargues. **Proprietor:** Comte A. de Lur Saluces. Production manager: Francis Mayeur. Vineyard manager Jacky Marquette. Cellar master: Guy Latrille. **Size of vineyard:** 12 hectares. **Average age of vines:** 23 years. **Varieties:** 20% sauvignon, 80% sémillon. **Production:** 5,000 bottles CB. **Sales by mail order:** in France. Château de Fargues, Fargues, 33210 Langon. Tel. 56 44 07 45. **Retail sales:** through Bordeaux.

"A proud castle in ruins, with a diminutive vineyard but the perfectionist standards of Yquem. Lighter wine, but impeccable and sometimes brilliant." So says Hugh Johnson in his *Wine Companion* (London, 1983). A systematic analysis of his judgement will help us to fix Fargues in time and space. Michel Piot, in his columns in *Le Figaro*, wrote that what Johnson writes in three lines takes me a whole book! Without wishing to contradict him, I will now simply comment on Hugh Johnson's superb British conciseness. "Impeccable and sometimes brilliant": the eulogy is brilliant but not entirely impeccable. If we wanted to be difficult, we could interpret it as a piece of flattery by a courtier whose discretion is more eloquent than the compliment itself. If we relate this definition to the terms which precede it, the exegesis becomes a doctrine of finality. With "the perfectionist standards of Yquem. Lighter wine". Here Johnson's message is clear: at Fargues, with the same "perfectionist standards", wines are made which will never be able to claim to rival Yquem. On this point, everyone will agree, or nearly everyone. If we compare entirely objectively the respective qualities of the 1981 vintage of Fargues and Yquem, we shall note

Behind the smoke of vine-prunings, Fargues bears witness to a warlike history.

the brilliant success of the former, particularly if we also take into consideration the sale price. For Fargues is about a third cheaper than its illustrious brother. Some claim that it is far too expensive for a *cru* which is not one of the *classés*! This said, Fargues has all the same a circle of devoted customers, so proving Alexandre de Lur Saluces entirely right. He is just as devoted to this ancient land of his ancestors (in their family since the marriage of Pierre de Lur and Isabeau de Montferrand in 1472) as to the incomparable terrain of Yquem which came as the dowry of Françoise-Joséphine de Sauvage on her marriage to Comte Louis-Amédée de Lur Saluces in 1785. So Fargues has been in the family for over three centuries longer than Yquem.

"With a diminutive vineyard. . . ", declares Hugh Johnson, and he is not wrong. A dozen hectares of vines will never make an ocean of sémillon! As to the viticultural references, not until the ninth edition of *Bordeaux et ses Vins*, in 1922, does Château de Fargues appear with its annual harvest of 50 *tonneaux* of "red wine", confirmed in the 1929 edition, and that of 1949. Twenty years later, Château de Fargues appears again to head the *Crus bourgeois supérieurs* in the twelfth edition "revised and enlarged" by Claude Féret. The thirteenth edition is decorated with an attractive design by Pierre Pagès, dated 1973, and we have the satisfaction of noting the appearance, in Fargues' entry, of a harvest of 25 *tonneaux* of white wine. Its place, "by order of merit", is third, following Rieussec and Romer. The text tells us that the history of Fargues dates from 1472, which as we have seen is correct as far as the history of the Lur Saluces family is concerned but which is rather ambiguous as to the viticultural origins of the *cru*. Two things appear to be certain: if the wines of Fargues were not under the aegis of Lur Saluces, they would not be rated so highly by public opinion, backed up by ready cash. But as they are indeed the work of Lur Saluces, they are duty bound to conform with the family's rigorous rules.

As to the "proud castle in ruins", time has left its mark. Built in 1306 by Cardinal Raimond-Guilhem de Fargues, the nephew of Pope Clement V, on the site of an old fortress, the château bears witness to a martial history appropriate to the ancient nobility of the Lurs and the Saluces. It is interesting to note that the Lur Saluces were also lords of Uza, in the Landes, where they owned huge smithies, still extant today. And the name Fargues has its etymology in these forges, as the priest Baurein tells us in his *Variétés bordelaises*. Today, the metal smelted at Fargues is gold, in liquid form.

Farluret (Château) ♀ ♀ ♀ ♀ ♀

Commune: Barsac. **Proprietors:** Robert Lamothe & Fils.
Size of vineyard: 8 hectares. **Average age of vines:** 50 years.
Varieties: 5% sauvignon, 90% sémillon, 5% muscadelle.
Production: 26,000 bottles CB. **Visits:** weekdays from
8 a.m. to noon and 2 to 6 p.m. Tel. 56 63 24 76. **Direct
sales and by mail order:** in France. Robert Lamothe, Haut-
Bergeron, Preignac, 33210 Langon. **Retail sales:** for export
only.

The Pontalies were a very ancient Barsac family, growers from father to son in the area of la Pinesse, to the south of the commune of Barsac. The Rivières have succeeded them and today it is Robert Lamothe who, by marriage, is lord of Farluret. This name has its origins in the Middle Ages when everybody was given a nickname. In about the thirteenth or fourteenth century, there is supposed to have been in the region a vigneron, a forester or a haymaker who was of rather feeble constitution but of vivacious character, called *Farluret*. The name has remained attached to the house where he lived and even today people still say in Barsac "I am off to Farluret ", that is, to the end of the commune beyond la Pinesse on the road leading to Pujols-sur-Ciron after crossing the motorway from les Deux-Mers. As for Robert Lamothe himself, he is unquestionably an "old Sauternian". His principal residence is at Preignac, where he also runs Château Haut-Bergeron (which has absolutely nothing to do with Lamothe-Bergeron at Cussac in the Upper Médoc). He likes to recall that in 1928, Farluret got the better of nearly all the great *crus classés* of Barsac. Nowadays, whenever it features at a tasting, this *cru* is placed in the top ranks most of the time. The 1985 is a very great wine, which is only beginning to unfold its aromas of crystallized fruit and toasted almonds. The 86 and 88 vintages follow in the same style. Farluret may be purchased with complete confidence.

Filhot (Château)

2e cru classé

Commune: Sauternes. **Proprietor:** G.F.A. du Château Filhot. Manager: Comte Henri de Vaucelles. Vineyard manager: Y. Gorry. Cellar master: P. Capbern. Consultant oenologist: J. Bouyx. **Size of vineyard:** 50 hectares. **Average age of vines:** 25 years. **Varieties:** 35% sauvignon, 60% sémillon, 5% muscadelle. **Production:** 110,000 bottles CB. **Visits:** weekdays from 8.30 a.m. to 12.30 p.m. and 2 to 6 p.m. H. de Vaucelles, tel. 56 63 61 09. **Direct sales and by mail order:** in France. G.F.A. du Château Filhot, Sauternes, 33210 Langon. **Retail sales:** Ets A. de Luze & Fils.

"*Sauternes.* The best wines belong to Monsieur Diquem, of Bordeaux or to Monsieur de Salus, his son-in-law; 150 *tonneaux* at 300 livres, young, and 600 livres, old. The next best *cru* is that of Monsieur Fillotte; 100 tonneaux, sold at the same price." This quotation from Thomas Jefferson's *Travel Notes* places Filhot in the lead among the great Sauternes wines as far back as the eighteenth century. A few years later, in 1816, Jullien published his *Topographie de tous les vignobles connus*: "The most famous *crus* are Clos Duroy, Ycum-Salus *(sic)* and Clos Fillot. Although their wines are all sold for the same price, the connoisseurs of the region draw fine distinctions between them and rate them in the order I have quoted." Here, Jullien seems to be confusing the old *cru* du Roy (or Pineau du Roy) with the *cru* Duroy in Preignac. The first was joined to Filhot after the 1855 classification by Romain-Bertrand, the Marquis of Lur Saluces.

I return to Jefferson to underline the pronunciation of the time, transcribed phonetically by the American: Fillotte. The Filhots acquired the property which today carries their name in 1709, that is about twenty years before the start of the "planting fever" which was to seize the Médoc and Graves. Severe frosts had destroyed the

vineyard. But the Filhots came from Quinsac, on the right bank of the Garonne, and were not familiar with the cold weather of Sauternes. Beginners' luck prevailed, for they had a run of good fortune: the arrival of the family from across the river turned out to be a success not only for them but for the whole Langon region because, from that moment on, the local climate improved for some time – almost until the end of the century. But in 1795, the frosts set in once more. However catastrophic this may have been, the change had providential consequences. Buyers of properties sequestered by the revolutionary government were in no hurry to invest in land

The Marquise de Lur Saluces,
née Caroline-Thérèse de Chastellux,
painted c 1840.

With 60 hectares under production, Filhot is one of the largest estates.

so capricious and cold. In 1806 Joséphine de Filhot, the Marquise de Lur Saluces, recovered her father's property at very little cost. Her husband, Napoleon I's chamberlain, even obtained a loan from Marshal Masséna to restore the vineyard. For the *cru* of Filhot, this meant the revival of its fame. From 1850 her son, Romain-Bertrand, quoted earlier, took the estate's fortunes in hand. The name "Filhot" then disappeared in favour of "Château de Sauternes". Meanwhile, other Sauternes wines proliferated and the uncontrolled appellation spread to nearby parishes and their surroundings. After half a century the term "Sauternes" was so debased that Filhot took on its former designation again. And that is why you can drink Château Filhot but cannot offer your guests Château de Sauternes, although it is the same wine.

As for their history and family reputation, the Filhots had no cause to envy the Lur Saluces. Their family was already renowned in the fifteenth century and was closely linked with the history of Guienne's Parlement. In the seventeenth century, Jacques de Filhot was chief treasurer and paymaster for France in the Bordeaux

region. During the "Ormée" revolt, he displayed remarkable devotion to the royal cause. The château of today, which many writers have dubbed a palace, was constructed in two different periods. The central section dates from the eighteenth century, whereas the wings were added by Romain-Bertrand de Lur Saluces in 1850 to designs drawn up by Poitevin. All the buildings together cover some two hectares of land. The estate's 330 hectares spread out over the entire breadth of the commune of Sauternes, from the Ciron to the forest of Fargues (the town hall is one of Filhot's old farm houses, held in *métayage*).

From 1870, farming activity declined in the southern half of the commune and the forest spread towards the vineyard, so increasing the risk of frost because of the stabilization of cold air. The size of the vineyard has varied considerably over the generations, from nothing right up to 120 hectares. At the moment, the size is maintained at 60 hectares. The Marquis Bertrand de Lur Saluces, the previous proprietor of Yquem, was also the master of Filhot from 1920 to 1935. He had his summer residence there. Those who benefited from his hospitality there at the time have memories of a princely establishment. But Filhot was far too large a dwelling for a person who intended to remain single. Bertrand de Lur Saluces shared his doubts with his sister, the wife of Comte Durieu de Lacarelle, and persuaded her to take over from him. Today, and since 1974, the G.F.A. du Château Filhot has been run by Comte Henri de Vaucelles.

Generally lighter and more sinewy than those of their great cousin Yquem, the wines of Filhot do not flaunt their richness. Rather they reveal a liveliness as delicate as it is marvellous. Never weighty or overbearing, they do not need to thrust themselves forward to display their breeding.

In the years with only a slight degree of botrytis, they tend to be dry yet retaining the hint of unctuousness which is expected of a well-born nectar. I personally prefer them in average years. They have a definite character, distinctive in comparison with their fellow *crus classés*. They have charm, and in great years, Filhot is a classic wine among many classics. But it will always retain that vivacity which is an essential part of its charm. Consider this, for example: in 1985, the fifth picking on the morning of November 23 was surreptitiously enriched by a sharp frost. Incidentally, I must say that I have always preferred the Filhot 1929 to the Yquem of the same year – and I speak from experience!

Fillau (Domaine de)

Commune: Fargues. **Proprietor:** Amédée Labarbe. **Size of vineyard:** 4.55 hectares. **Average age of vines:** 35 years. **Varieties:** 15% sauvignon, 80% sémillon, 5% muscadelle. **Production:** 12 *tonneaux* 4,500 bottles CB. **Direct sales and by mail order:** Amédée Labarbe, au Bourg, Fargues, 33210 Langon. Tel 56 63 09 92. *This estate produces a supple, agreeable wine which can be drunk easily and leaves the palate fresh and clean.*

Gilette (Château)

Commune: Preignac. **Proprietor:** Christian Médeville. **Size area of vineyard:** 4.5 hectares. **Average age of vines:** 35 years. **Varieties:** 15% sauvignon, 83% sémillon, 2% muscadelle. **Production:** 6 *tonneaux*, 6,000 bottles C B. **Visits:** Monday to Friday from 9 a.m. to 6 p.m.; groups are requested to make a prior appointment. Tel. 56 63 27 59. **Direct sales and by mail order:** in France. Monsieur Christian Médeville, "L'Antiquaire de Sauternes", 33210 Preignac. **Retail sales:** only a small proportion of the production is sold to the trade.

Unique throughout Bordeaux, the wines of Christian Médeville are aged for nearly twenty years before being offered for sale. This is not through caprice but is a deliberate policy on the part of the proprietor who likes to call himself "the antique dealer of Sauternes". His range of vintages is firmly fixed in past years and, if you want Sauternes "en primeur" it is definitely not at the door of his cellar that you should knock. On the other hand, he can offer you (though only drop by drop) his "crème de tête" of the years 1947, '53 or '55 (when Elvis Presley was making his first

Jean Médeville, Christian's great-grandfather, surveys the upkeep of the cellar.

record in Memphis!), made from grapes harvested by René Médeville, Christian's father, in seven runs, resulting in the divine nectar which is now ready to grace the table of a few fortunate wine lovers.

For the Médevilles, Sauternes is a love story. They have been in the parish of Preignac from 1710 (see Château Les Justices). Gilette is the standard-bearer of their range, of which none reveals the slightest evidence of laxness. For generation after generation, they have attracted a really special clientele including the greatest restaurateurs, like acolytes handing on the religion of good drinking from father to son. By the side of the aristocracy of the Barsac great *crus*, the Médevilles in my view represent the archetype of "meritocracy". Gilette 1955, *cuvée* "crème de tête": a superb, transparent golden yellow colour, prodigious bouquet whose complex ethers you never tire of analysing and which yet remains extremely difficult to describe, all words seeming inadequate. On the palate, there is volume and a magnificent fullness with no false note whatever. In other words, this is a wine which makes you close your eyes and induces a reverent silence.

Grand Mayne (Château) ☖ → Simon

Gravas (Château)

Commune: Barsac. **Proprietor** and director: Pierre Bernard. Consultant oenologist: Albert Bouyx. **Size of vineyard:** 10 hectares. **Varieties:** 10% sauvignon, 80% sémillon, 10% muscadelle. **Production:** 33,000 bottles CB. **Visits:** possible everyday from 9 a.m. to noon and 2 to 7 p.m. **Direct sales and by mail order:** in France and abroad. Pierre Bernard, Château Gravas, Barsac, 33720 Podensac. Tel. 56 27 15 20.

After the 1855 classification, the *cru* of Doisy was split into three. From the 1860s onwards, there were three growers, using the names Doisy Daenne, Doisy-Védrines and Doisy-Gravas. The first two came directly from the *cru classé*, and the third, listed by Cocks and Féret in 1868 with the good *crus bourgeois*, then belonged to the Saint-Cyr-Debans family. After this, the name disappeared for about twenty years. In 1922, *Bordeaux et ses Vins* mentions only the *"cru* de Gravas", producing 6 *tonneaux* per year and belonging to Claverie. Gravas is a small place near Barsac, situated halfway between Coutet and Climens. Its *cru* status was confirmed in 1929, and in 1949 Cocks and Féret's eleventh edition mentions Château Gravas for the first time. Following on from Claverie, Pierre Bernard claims a staggering past: "The fame of Château Gravas goes back to the time of Richard the Lionheart (twelfth century)." At that time, however, Yquem itself did not exist! But there is no need of such myths to prove that good wine is made here. Château Gravas features very honourably among middle-range Barsacs. One should not expect any strokes of genius from this wine, but rather a pleasing constancy in quality. That being said, the wine lover will always find it good value for money.

Grillon (Château)

Commune: Barsac. **Proprietor:** Madame Roumazeilles-Cameleyre. Consultant oenologist: M. Gendrot. **Size of vineyard:** 11 hectares. **Average age of vines:** 40 years. **Varieties:** 10% sauvignon, 75% sémillon, 15% muscadelle. **Production:** 36,000 bottles CB. **Visits:** daily until 7 p.m. Tel. 56 27 16 45. **Direct sales and by mail order:** in France. Madame Roumazeilles-Cameleyre, Château Grillon, Barsac, 33720 Podensac. **Retail sales.**

In the last quarter of the nineteenth century, Edouard Féret, after breaking his ties with Charles Cocks, assumed a place of major importance in the field of administrative and economic information in the *département* of the Gironde. Following the book which was to become famous, *Bordeaux et ses Vins, classés par ordre de mérite*, he produced his more systematic *Statistique de la Gironde*, making use of the works of Jouanet, published between 1835 and 1845. Twenty years after the 1855 classification, the title of *cru classé* did not have all the historical and prestigious connotation which it has today. So the boundary between the last on the list of *crus classés* and the first of the *crus bourgeois* had to be revised from time to time, from vintage to vintage and from one *cru* to another. The brokers and the merchants of the Chartrons judged the quality of the wines with the indisputable authority of those who know and who pay. Despite the prestige of any particular name (authentic labels of any *cru* were then very unusual), a flavour of acidity or must, any sickliness or bitterness, or any thin or vinegary taste would be damned with a fall in prices which could sometimes be very considerable. Oenology was not what it is today and accidents were far from rare. Hampered by price fluctuations which showed theoretically inexplicable divergences from the fixed average, Edouard Féret had to review the positions of the *crus classés par ordre de mérite* with each new edition. Of course he did not interfere too much with the higher echelons. Depending on the transient success of the moment (or the nature of his relations with the proprietors), he might quote such and such a *cru* before another in spite of the official order in the classification (for example, Caillou before Doisy in the 1874 edition). Naturally, he had to face numerous criticisms, complaints and objections. So he adopted a "composite" heading under which the *deuxièmes crus* were amalgamated with the *crus bourgeois supérieurs*. The order of presentation might well be modified between two editions, but all the vineyards of these categories were to be found under the same heading. This is how Château Grillon came to be included under the heading *Deuxièmes crus* or *Bourgeois supérieurs*" from 1874 and in successive editions. At the very beginning of the century, Elie Plomby, the proprietor of Grillon, had an elegant label printed which read *Château Grillon, 2e cru classé*. This practice came to an end a few years later when the Federation of Sauternes and Barsac *crus classés* decided that Grillon was wrongly making use of a status it had never had. Following this, Féret listed the *crus classés* and the *crus bourgeois* separately. I have taken the case of Château Grillon here simply as an example, but it is typical of the spell cast by the mantra "*cru classé*" on all growers of every generation.

2ᵐᵉ CRU CLASSÉ

Elie Plomby bought the estate in 1903, when the name already had an excellent reputation. He had to sell it twenty-three years later to Henri Cameleyre, a shipowner in Arcachon. The description of the assets, as they feature in the deeds, gives a rapid general sketch: "Principal dwelling, workers' dwellings, several other buildings such as sheds, bake house, stables and other constructions, garden, land, vines, meadows and heathland, hornbeams, acacias and others, the whole representing a total of approximately seventeen hectares". The different varieties of crops should be noted. Mixed farming was then more common than today. To give an idea of the equipment on the estate, here is the list drawn up by the notary under the incorrect heading "fixtures": "one mare for different purposes – one cart – one tip-cart – one waggon with sulphating vat – one mobile sulphating machine – three portable sulphating sprays – two sulphur pulverizers – one Pilter plough – one ploughshare – two harrows – one rotating harrow – one scraper". The wine-making installations must have been scanty, for Elie Plomby had the vat-house and cellars entirely re-equipped at his own cost before selling the property to Henri Cameleyre.

Madame Odile Roumazeilles, née Cameleyre, is the owner of Château Grillon today. Do not question her too closely about late harvesting and staggered selective pickings: she simply sides with the majority of those who practise them, and to justify them, she refers to the story previously mentioned of the Marquis Romain-Bertrand de Lur Saluces returning home one month late after a hunting party in Russia. At Grillon, blind faith makes delicious wine.

Guiraud (Château)

1er cru classé

Commune: Sauternes. **Proprietor:** S.C.A. du Château Guiraud. Director: Hamilton Narby. Estate manager: Xavier Planty. Vineyard manager: Jacky Eymmery. Cellar master: Roland Dubile. Consultant oenologist: M. Chauvet. **Size of vineyard:** 118 hectares. **Average age of vines:** 25 years. **Varieties:** 45% sauvignon, 54% sémillon, 1% muscadelle. **Production:** 100,000 bottles CB. **Visits:** daily from 9 a.m. to noon and 2.30 to 6 p.m. Tel. 56 63 61 01. **Direct sales and by mail order:** in France. S.C.A. du Château Guiraud, Sauternes, 33210 Langon. **Retail sales.**

"Still leading his horse, Monsieur Poncet-Deville continued in his engaging role as guide.

'On the right', he said, 'you can see a modest little château, between Yquem and the village of Sauternes. It is Château Guiraud, a Sauternes *Premier Cru*. It belongs now to Monsieur Bernard, a fine man who, like his predecessors, continues to keep his vines in good shape and to make excellent wine. At the time when Monsieur

At the time of the 1855 classification, Guiraud was known as Bayle.

Mirès had achieved the peak of prosperity, Monsieur Félix Solar bought Château Guiraud from him, convinced that an exceptional future was assured for the area as a result of the opening up of new means of communications. Monsieur Félix was a connoisseur of everything, literature, fine food and excellent wine; he had stocked his cellar with the greatest care and attention, as well as his library. Consequently he had a great number of friends who arrived in droves to visit him, to look with curiosity at his handsomely bound books about the greatest *crus*, and to dip into his precious bottles. But one day, a black cloud darkened the horizon and a fierce wind blew over Monsieur Solar, his fortune, his books, his bottles and his château. It also blew away his friends, who disappeared like startled crows.

'The proprietor, who knew his letters, could have said, like the Roman poet in the country where he was to die:

> *donec eris Felix, multos numerabis amicos.*
> *tempora si fuerint nubila, Solar eris. . .*

And that is how Château Guiraud passed from Solar to Bernard. As for the wine, there is no cause for worry: it continues to be one of the best.' "

This extract from the *Voyage autour des vins de France*, written in 1878 by Bertall, is a nice illustration of the many vicissitudes through which Sauternes château owners passed. This *cru* has known its days of glory and nights of despair. When in July 1981 Hamilton Narby, standing guarantee for his family, bought the great estate of nearly 120 hectares, the condition of the vineyard and cellars and the *cru*'s reputation had seriously declined. The Narbys are of Canadian origin.

Hamilton Narby.

Over the generations, exploiting wind and tide, this family of shipowners amassed a huge fortune. Hamilton Narby has placed the family escutcheon on Guiraud's label, convinced that the dolphin will serve as a mascot to bring good luck to his wine. This stylish symbol has proved an emblem of Guiraud's rebirth. For in a very short time, the whole of the estate had been put back into shape. The first great reward was the 1983 vintage. "Sheer glory for Guiraud", Hamilton Narby declares calmly, "we finished harvesting on November 28 in Utopian conditions! It is the best wine we have made ... until the '88." As he utters these words, the shipowner's grandson looks rather as Aladdin must have done when he realized what he had found in his cave.

Geographically Guiraud is, in the manner of Yquem, the only *Premier Cru* to be wholly in the commune of Sauternes. The slopes of its vineyard look down on the little village and roll gently down towards the Ciron. In its gravelly, siliceous and clayey land, drainage takes place naturally and cultivation presents no particular problems. The vines are favourably exposed. There is no doubt that the great vessel "Guiraud" is built and equipped for high-class business. Hamilton Narby also likes luxury cars: "With Yquem Sauternes has a Rolls-Royce, and Guiraud is its Bentley." Land, sea and air – for we should not forget that ballooning is among the favourite pastimes of this gentleman farmer. In high season, you can also make an appointment to fly silently over the beautiful countryside of Sauternes in the proprietor's hot-air balloon. This is complete escape, to float dreamlike among the birds. As if by magic, the gods carry you into the skies from where you look down on the earth, gleaming in the golden light of Sauternes, like a fabled land.

Coming back to earth, we find sauvignon vines basking contentedly in the midday sun after a Turkish bath in the morning mist of the Ciron. Guiraud is the *cru classé* with the highest percentage of sauvignon. This is not what is really responsible for its splendour; it rather gives the wines an individual character. They have that fruity stamina which is so typical of this grape. Hamilton Narby takes his glass between his thumb and forefinger. He holds it up to the light to admire the gold colour and he gently swirls the wine in the glass. His nose then captures the object of his desire. He closes his eyes. You can no longer see him breathing. He inhales pure ecstasy. You think he has finished. He takes a sip. The tiniest sip. You can see the veins throb in his temples. He is analysing Guiraud. You almost feel you should not be there. Finally he swallows and, as if he had just landed in his balloon, and is seeing you for the first time: "What fine body!", he says smiling.

Guiteronde du Hayot (Château)

Commune: Barsac. **Proprietor:** G.F.A. du Hayot. Consultant oenologist: Albert Bouyx. **Size of vineyard:** 30 hectares. **Average age of vines:** 25 years. **Varieties:** 25% sauvignon, 65% sémillon, 10% muscadelle. **Production:** 90,000 bottles CB. **Visits:** from Monday to Friday. Tel. 56 27 15 37. **Direct sales and by mail order:** in France and abroad. G.F.A. du Hayot, Barsac, 33720 Podensac. **Retail sales**.

The Journus, an old Aquitaine family, were proprietors of this *cru* at the beginning of the nineteenth century. In his 1850 edition, Charles Cocks cites thirty-one *crus* in Barsac. Guitte-Ronde (the old spelling) was nineteenth on this list. The financial group, the G.F.A. du Hayot, owns several small or average-sized estates in Barsac. Guiteronde du Hayot is the largest with its 30 hectares of vines. The other labels to be found are Brassens-Guiteronde, Camperos and Pebayle. This is a convenient diversification for relatively large-scale production which is distributed to the market through various chains. With an average annual yield of 25 to 30 hectolitres per hectare the Hayot group qualifies for an entry in the record books. Were it a *grand cru classé* of the Médoc, these would not be exceptional figures, but these yields are generous from a terrain consecrated to under-production in order to aim for the highest quality.

Haire (Château du)

Commune: Preignac. **Proprietor** and director: Jean-Pierre Cartier. Consultant oenologist: Albert Bouyx. **Size of vineyard:** 5.2 hectares. **Average age of vines:** 30 years. **Varieties:** 15% sauvignon, 75% sémillon, 10% muscadelle. **Production:** 14 *tonneaux,* 17,000 bottles CB. **Direct sales and by mail order:** in France. Monsieur Cartier, Château du Haire, Preignac, 33210 Langon. Tel. 56 63 41 73. **Retail sales:** through the trade.

Jean-Pierre Cartier is close to celebrating his family's centenary in the area of le Haire, and with it fifty years of château bottling: indeed, the estate has been handed down from father to son since 1896. Today this *cru* is entirely given over to selling its wines in bottle with the *cru*'s attractive label (slightly old-fashioned but gently nostalgic). The various plots which make up the vineyard are spread out over the choicest land, between Preignac and Sauternes, some of them lying on a gentle gravelly slope in the commune of Sauternes. The name "Haire" unites them all in one wine. The etymology of this little, ancient locality in Preignac is disputed. For some, Haire means a fair or a market, coming from the Gascon word *hère*. For others, it comes from the old French word *here*, in the sense of master, and means heir. Whatever the case, the quality of Jean-Pierre Cartier's wines is not a matter of dispute.

Haut-Bergeron (Château) ♀ ♀ ♀ ♀ ♀

Commune: Preignac. **Proprietor:** Robert Lamothe & Fils. **Size of vineyard:** 11.5 hectares. **Average age of vines:** 60 years. **Varieties:** 5% sauvignon, 90% sémillon, 5% muscadelle. **Production:** 36,000 bottles CB. **Visits:** Weekdays from 8 a.m. to noon and 2 to 6 p.m. Tel. 56 63 24 76. **Direct sales and by mail order:** in France. Robert Lamothe, Haut-Bergeron, Preignac, 33210 Langon. **Retail sales:** abroad.

The Lamothe family has been in the Sauternes region since the seventeenth century. Robert and Hervé Lamothe are diligent growers and careful vintners, motivated by a constant desire to produce wine of the highest quality. The fruit of their labours has already been recognized and hailed by many enlightened wine lovers. Here I should mention the discovery of this wine by Jean-Paul Kauffmann, the journalist with *L'Evénement du Jeudi* who was for three years a hostage* in the Lebanon. In *L'Amateur de Bordeaux* (a quarterly review edited by him), this is how he describes his discovery:

"In 1941, Prunier's restaurant supplied Colonel Rémy with six bottles of Sauternes for members of the crew of a German submarine based in Lorient. Thanks to the effects produced by these precious wines, the secret agent Alphonse Tanguy managed to spirit away the German defence plans. Thirty years later Marcel Achard, recalling this exploit at Prunier's, awarded a symbolic 'Order of the Nation' to Châteaux Filhot, Suduiraut, La Tour Blanche, and Piada. And Haut-Bergeron. He also dubbed Yquem Compagnon de la Libération.

Château Haut-Bergeron has retained its reputation. Awarded four medals for its 1982 vintage, this *cru*, whose vines are next to those of the prestigious Château d'Yquem, made special mention on its label of being 'next door to Yquem': a geographical privilege which is not solely responsible for Haut-Bergeron's success. For three generations, the Lamothes have maintained the fame of this Sauternes with the discretion and restraint of a family business. Robert Lamothe, his wife and their son Hervé, a qualified young oenologist, helped by three families, look after the estate. They are particularly careful with harvesting, which they entrust only to local people, for Robert Lamothe considers that three years' experience is needed to know how to gather the grapes individually. Already the 1982 vintage has a fine harmony of aromas: hints of cinnamon, honey and cider can be detected. Its richness in sugar does not mask its finesse. Rich and distinguished, it lingers on the palate with a hint of walnut. This Haut-Bergeron should reach its peak in about 1995. None the less, Robert Lamothe considers it can be drunk even now, for the muscadelle gives this young Sauternes a slight touch of 'rancio', as found in the very oldest vintages. The breeding and elegance of this wine, which can rival many *crus classés* and even outshine some, show that in Sauternes great wines can be produced even without the

*Jean-Paul Kauffmann was freed on May 5, 1988 after being held in captivity for 1,078 days.

privilege of featuring in the classification which has influenced the better judgement of more than one taster. By his determination and rigour, Robert Lamothe does honour to a name which has not always lived up to its reputation."

Haut-Bommes (Château)

Commune: Bommes. **Proprietor:** G.F.A. du Clos Haut-Peyraguey. Director and cellar master: Jacques Pauly. Consultant oenologist: Pierre Sudraud. **Size of vineyard:** 6 hectares. **Average age of vines:** 35 years. **Varieties:** 15% sauvignon, 85% sémillon. **Production:** 16,000 bottles CB. **Visits:** Groups are requested to make prior appointment. Jacques Pauly, tel. 56 63 61 53. **Direct sales and by mail order:** in France. G.F.A. du Clos Haut-Peyraguey, Bommes, 33210 Langon. **Retail sales:** occasionally abroad.

Eugène Garbay was mayor of Bommes and director of Château La Tour Blanche. In 1926 he bequeathed to Pierre and Bernard Pauly, his grandsons, this modest estate which had been created, plot by plot, over the generations since the beginning of the eighteenth century.

It lies principally between Rayne Vigneau and La Tour Blanche. The term "Haut-Bommes" is quite accurate, since the vineyard lies at one of the highest points in the commune (between 45 and 65 metres high). The dwelling is a pleasant country house, surrounded by well-kept outbuildings. I do not know how Jacques Pauly – who has been running the estate since 1969 – divides his wines between the names "Haut-Bommes" and "Haut-Peyraguey" (q.v.). But overall his wines reach a very honourable level of quality, even if Haut-Bommes is in truth the second wine of Clos Haut-Peyraguey.

Haut-Claverie (Domaine du)

Commune: Fargues. **Proprietor:** G.F.A. Domaine du Haut-Claverie. Managed by: G.A.E.C. Sendrey Frères et Fils. Consultant oenologist: Jean-Paul Pauquet. **Size of vineyard:** 11 hectares. **Average age of vines:** 25 years. **Varieties:** 10% sauvignon, 85% sémillon, 5% muscadelle. **Production:** 30 *tonneaux*,15,000 bottles CB. **Visits:** tastings and sales everyday, preferably by appointment. Sendrey Frères et Fils, tel. 56 63 12 65. **Direct sales and by mail order:** in France. G.A.E.C. Sendrey Frères et Fils, Fargues, 33210 Langon. **Retail sales:** Maison de Luze, Bordeaux.

The ancestors of the Sendreys were called "Claveries". They gave their name to this hamlet in the commune of Fargues whose summit lies at a height of about 75 metres. There is documentary evidence of their presence here since 1800. Bernard, Michel and Philippe Sendrey dutifully continue the family tradition. The Domaine du Haut Claverie produces excellent, occasionally magnificent, wines which can be bought with complete confidence.

Haut-Lagueritte (Cru) ♟ → La Gauche

Haut Mayne (Château)

Commune: Barsac. **Proprietor:** Madame Joseph Bravo. **Directors:** Madame Pierre and Monsieur J.-B. Bravo. **Consultant oenologists:** M. Llorca and M. Peynaud. **Size of vineyard:** 3.34 hectares. **Average age of vines:** 25 years. **Varieties:** 5% sauvignon, 95% sémillon. **Production:** 9,000 bottles CB. **Direct sales and by mail order:** Madame Joseph Bravo, Ch. Caillou, Barsac, 33720 Podensac. Tel. 56 27 16 38. **Retail sales.**

This attractive little estate, in the neighbourhood of Château Coutet, has a pleasant dwelling and a spacious garden. It belongs to the Bravo family which owns Château Caillou through the female line. Vinified and aged in the cellars of Caillou, the wine of Haut Mayne appears as a second label of the *cru classé* (the same applies to Château Petit Mayne).

Haut-Violet (Château) ♟ → Monteils

Jacques le Haut (Château) ♟ → Mont-Joye

Janonier (Domaine)

Commune: Bommes. **Proprietor:** Yvon Pouyaud. **Size of vineyard:** 2.6 hectares. **Average age of vines:** 25 years. **Varieties:** 25% sauvignon, 50% sémillon, 25% muscadelle. **Production:** 6 *tonneaux*. **Direct sales:** Yvon Pouyaud, Bommes, 33210 Langon. Tel. 56 63 65 24. **Retail sales:** in bulk. *A very small quantity is bottled on the estate to meet the needs of local customers.*

Jany (Château)

Commune: Barsac. **Proprietor:** Huguette Estrade (Estrade family trust). Tenant and cellar master: Bertrand Turtaut. **Size of vineyard:** 3.5 hectares. **Average age of vines:** 80 years. **Varieties:** 20% sauvignon, 70% sémillon, 10% muscadelle. **Production:** 10 *tonneaux*, 4,000 bottles CB. **Visits:** by appointment. Tel. 56 27 03 26. **Direct sales and by mail order:** Bertrand Turtaut, Pleguemate, Barsac, 33720 Podensac. **Retail sales:** approximately two thirds of the production is sold in bulk to the trade.

These are certainly some of the oldest vines in the Sauternes region: the part of the vineyard lying along the R.N. 113, is more than a hundred years old. The property was bought in about 1900 by the Estrade family, from Corrèze. Both father and son knew how to get the best out of. They went to sell their wine themselves in Belgium and northern France. But the son, Jean Estrade, had four daughters, none of whom showed any inclination for growing or marketing. So in 1959 he decided to rent his estate to André Turtaut. The latter's widow, Madame Odette Turtaut continued the work of her late husband until her own recent death. After working for seventeen years alongside his parents, Bertrand Turtaut, who also works 15 hectares in Barsac, has taken up the torch. The late Madame Turtaut sold most of her harvest in bulk but had a sure touch when it came to selecting the wines to be bottled at the château. She had her own personal ideas about the quality of the Barsac wines from year to year. Here is her – and her son's – own vintage chart rating out of 20 the last twenty-five years.

1988	19	1983	18	1978	18	1973	14	1968	0
1987	18	1982	19.5	1977	0	1972	0	1967	15.5
1986	15	1981	19.5	1976	19.5	1971	15.5	1966	17.5
1985	17	1980	16	1975	19.5	1970	18	1965	0
1984	16	1979	18	1974	15	1969	0	1964	0

Jauga (Château) ☫ → Rabaud-Promis

Jean Blanc (Château) ☫ → Sigalas Rabaud

Jouanous (Domaine des) ♟♟♟♟♟

Commune: Sauternes. **Proprietor:** Guy Ducos, Nautet, Sauternes, 33210 Langon. Tel. 56 62 31 56. **Size of vineyard:** 2 hectares. **Average age of vines:** 30 years. **Production:** 4 *tonneaux*. **Retail sales:** in bulk.

sold in bulk

Juge (Château du) ♟♟♟♟♟

Commune: Preignac. **Proprietor:** Madame Françoise Guix de Pinos, Preignac, 33210 Langon. Tel. 56 63 22 11. **Size of vineyard:** 4 hectares. **Average age of vines:** 30 years. **Varieties:** 20% sauvignon, 80% sémillon. **Production:** 11 *tonneaux*. **Retail sales:** the entire production is sold in bulk through the Bordeaux trade.

sold in bulk

During the Revolution and the Reign of Terror, just like in the Wild West in its most heroic period, a Justice of the Peace settled in Preignac. History has not recorded his name for us, but has left us merely the evidence of his high office in the name of this *cru* and that of the" Château des Justices" (as if there had ever been several kinds of justice). The Juge estate lies at the very heart of the residential area of Preignac is one single stretch; the vineyard is planted on sandy soil with a low gravel content. It is not the early morning mists from the Ciron which encourage *Botrytis cinerea* here 125 but those from the Garonne. (What matter where they come from provided the rot be noble!) The foundations of the house at Juge go back to the Middle Ages. The central body of the building was restyled in the time of Louis XIII. The wings date from the eighteenth century. This property was bought in 1876 by Eugène Plantey, the maternal great-grandfather of the present owner, Madame Françoise Guix de Pinos. In 1911 the vineyard was enlarged by the addition of a plot taken from Château d'Armajan des Ormes. It is highly regrettable that the wine of Château du Juge is handled in bulk. It would do justice to itself to imprison the best of its production in bottle.

L'Abeilley (Clos) 🍷 → *Rayne Vigneau*

Labère (Clos) 🍷 → *Rieussec*

La Chapelle Saint-Antoine 🍷
→ *La Chapelle Saint-Aubin*

La Chapelle Saint-Aubin   ♀ ♀ ♀ ♀ ♀

Commune: Bommes. **Proprietor:** Jean-Louis Dubos. Consultant oenologist: Albert Bouyx. **Size of vineyard:** 4.5 hectares. **Average age of vines:** 30 to 40 years. **Varieties:** 20% sauvignon, 70% sémillon, 10% muscadelle. **Production:** 12 *tonneaux*, 5,000 to 6,000 bottles CB. **Visits:** by appointment. Jean-Louis Dubos, tel. 56 63 63 25. **Direct sales and by mail order:** in France. Jean-Louis Dubos, La Chapelle Saint-Aubin, Bommes, 33210 Langon. **Retail sales:** through the trade and to private clients (see text).

Jean-Louis Dubos has two chapels: "Saint-Antoine", which enables him to invoice his sales in bulk to the trade, and "Saint-Aubin", which adorns the label destined for his château-bottled wines. Be this as it may, an air of genuine sanctity reigns over the estates. The present cellar-cum-vat-house was a religious building founded by the Feuillants. The patron saint was certainly Saint Anthony, since the Order of the Hospices of the Antonins (or Antonists) was created in the thirteenth century in an endeavour to treat Saint Anthony's fire, otherwise called "the rose" or erysipelas

(see the volume on Saint-Estèphe in this collection). As for Saint Aubin, a chapel situated at the north-eastern end of the parish of Bommes was dedicated to him. If the wine lover is at his wits' end or, as we say in French, does not know which saint to pray to, I urge him to turn his attentions to the label of Saint-Aubin.

La Chartreuse (Château) 🛡 → *Saint-Amand*

La Côte (Domaine de) 🍷🍷🍷🍷🍷

Commune: Fargues. **Proprietor:** Marc Lasserre. **Size of vineyard:** 3.8 hectares. **Average age of vines:** 35 years. **Varieties:** 15% sauvignon, 80% sémillon, 5% muscadelle. **Production:** 8 *tonneaux*, 800 bottles CB. **Direct sales and by mail order:** in France. Marc Lasserre, Au bourg, Fargues, 33210 Langon. Tel. 56 63 51 05. **Retail sales:** S.I.C.A. Sauternes Barsac.

Sadly Monsieur and Madame Marc Lasserre are well aware that their children do not want to carry on with the estate after them. And yet it is well situated, with several plots round the village of Fargues and in the area of les Claveries. The family has been here for three generations living in the former presbitery. Niches in the wall used to shelter religious statues. The house has a vaulted cellar which is undoubtedly extremely ancient in origin.

Because of the quantity of work it implies ,the Lasserres do a very small amount of château bottling but they choose the quality of the wine for this with the greatest of care. Their label should attract the attention of collectors for it is unquestionably one of the rarest in Sauternes. Any bottle bearing it may be counted upon to contain delicious nectar *à l'ancienne*.

Lafaurie-Peyraguey (Château) 🍷🍷🍷🍷🍷

1er cru classé

Commune: Bommes. **Proprietor:** Domaines Cordier. Estate manager and cellar master: M. Laporte. Manager and consultant oenologist: M. Pauli. **Size of vineyard:** 27 hectares. **Average age of vines:** 30 years. **Varieties:** 15% sauvignon, 80% sémillon, 5% muscadelle. **Production:** *50 tonneaux* 60,000 bottles CB. **Visits:** by appointment from Monday to Friday from 8 a.m. to noon and 2 p.m. to 5.30 p.m. Tel. 56 31 44 44. **Sales by mail order:** in France and abroad (through agents). Etablissements Cordier, 10 quai de Paludate, 33800 Bordeaux. **Retail sales:** exclusively through Etablissements Cordier.

Enclosed by castellated walls, and flanked by corner towers and ornamented with a variety of windows, this château was constructed on the plan of a mediaeval fortress. The entrance, a great covered archway, gives access to an inner courtyard dominated by a rectangular keep with watchtower and machicolations. The main body of the building seems to have been rebuilt in the seventeenth century and

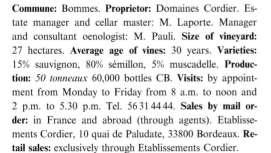

As with all the Cordier estates, Lafaurie-Peyraguey is impeccably kept.

it is obvious that the whole of it was radically altered during the last century. Its architecture is rather unusual: "Seen from afar, this curious arrangement of tulip-shaped arches, oriental windows and white defensive walls is evocative of the areas round Seville or Granada at the time of the Saracens", notes Charles Dormontal; and Bertall is rather derisory: "It is a mosque, a harem, a palace if you wish. But, by Mohammed, it is not a château! With a few sultans and a passable number of negresses following them down the walks, sheltering them with huge red and gold parasols, it would be a wonderful sight. But there are no palm trees." And he continues his mockery with the declaration that the cellar master ought to wear a turban and an arab cloak in order to resemble "the Turkish sweet-seller at the Palais-Royal". Finally, he concludes: "All the same, save for the palm trees and the sultans, it is true that this dwelling is a charming fantasy worthy to receive Aaroun-al-Rothschild who, we are told, sometimes comes here with Goudal, his vizier, when the pasha, the proprietor of the palace, is spending some time in the region." At the time when Bertall was writing, the proprietor of Lafite was Baron James de Rothschild, seconded by his excellent" business adviser", Emile Goudal, who had some influence on the viticulture of the Gironde. As for the pasha, the proprietor of Lafaurie-Peyraguey, this was Comte Duchâtel who, was Minister of the Interior under Louis-Philippe and who also owned Château Lagrange at Saint-Julien. Peyraguey (for this was how it was known at the end of the nineteenth century) formerly belonged to Saint-Rieul-Dupouy, a writer and journalist with the *Courrier de la Gironde*, to whom we owe in particular a delightful article entitled *L'Eté à Bordeaux*. He had acquired the property in 1864 from the widow of Lafaurie. Writers of the period report that the vineyard was superbly well cultivated, producing around 65 *tonneaux* a year, which implies that the estate was larger than it is today.

Georges Pauli.

It had been created in the eighteenth century by a magistrate, M. de Pichard, the president of the Parlement in Bordeaux, who was later guillotined during the Reign of Terror. Lafaurie acquired it when the property was sequestered by the Revolutionary government, and proved himself a first-class viticulturalist. For a time the *cru* was called "Pichard-Lafaurie". It was the favourite wine of His Catholic Majesty King Alphonse XII of Spain, who bought a hogshead of 1858 for 6,000 gold francs, that is 24,000 francs per *tonneau!* Thus the price paid for 1847 Yquem by the Grand Duke Constantine of Russia – 20,000 francs per *tonneau* – was beaten. On June 26, 1879, Farinel and Grédy became the proprietors of Peyraguey by disinheriting the heirs of Count Duchâtel. Their mother had already split off the part of the vineyard called "Clos Haut-Peyraguey" (see above). It was in 1913 that Désiré Cordier (see our volume on Saint-Julien) became the owner of the estate. Since then it has been run by the firm of Cordier under the meticulous and competent direction of Georges Pauli, whose merits I have often had occasion to praise.

The vineyard was enlarged by four and a half hectares in 1980 by the acquisition of a plot from Château d'Arche. Georges Pauli's relentless logic and sure instinct allow him to combine traditional methods of agronomy and oenology with modern ones. He keeps the yield down to less than two *tonneaux* per hectare. Fermentation takes place in the wood but it is arrested, when the required degree of alcohol is attained, by the smallest amount of sulphur dioxide with the addition of thiamine (vitamin B) to restrict the extent to which the sulphur can combine. Cold treatment ensures clarification, and the wine does not undergo any further massive doses of sulphur. All this is not mere chemistry when it it is a question of wine: on the contrary, it represents an intelligent use of progress. The Lafaurie-Peyragueys are very great Sauternes which I currently rate with the very best. Recent vintages, even the 1984 – an off-year if ever these was one – , are superb. The 88 probably rates among the greatest wines ever produced here.

Lafon (Château)

Commune: Sauternes. **Proprietor:** Jean-Pierre Dufour. Consultant oenologist: Pierre Sudraud. **Size of vineyard:** 6 hectares. **Average age of vines:** 35 years. **Varieties:** 8% sauvignon, 89% sémillon, 3% muscadelle. **Production:** 16 *tonneaux*, 1,500 bottles CB. **Direct sales and by mail order:** in France. Jean-Pierre Dufour, Château Lafon, Sauternes, 33210 Langon. Tel. 56 63 30 82. **Retail sales:** Maison Dourthe, Parempuyre.

Those who are happy have no history, and the privileged sémillon vines of Château Lafon, dotted here and there with a few sauvignon and muscadelle vines, live peacefully in the midst of their regal Yquem equivalents. Jean-Pierre Dufour's grandfather

Jean-Pierre Dufour in his vineyard, with Château d'Yquem on the horizon.

bought this little jewel of a vineyard in 1938. Since then, nothing has changed much either in the vineyard or in the buildings, among which an attractive little house of romantic charm catches the eye.

The wines of Château Lafon are thoroughly classic. Jean-Pierre Dufour likes to classify them in two groups: not good and bad, which would be a Manichaean over-simplification, but "fruity" and "ripe". To a long story short, the fruity ones are those which are ripe and the ripe ones are those which are more than ripe. To inject a little subtlety into this distinction, you could say that the fruity ones may be sturdy and fruity or extremely fruity and the ripe ones subdivide into slightly over-ripe and extremely over-ripe. The wine lover should certainly enjoy discovering the delicate nuances within each group. For thirty years now the dependable firm of Dourthe has distributed both the ripe and the fruity wines of Lafon. This reciprocal fidelity between both producer and distributor is testimony to the happy working relationship that has been established by these two partners.

La Garenne (Château)   ♟ ♟ ♟ ♟ ♟

Commune: Preignac. **Proprietors:** Jean-Pierre Ferbos & Fils. **Size of vineyard:** 5 hectares. **Average age of vines:** 20 years. **Varieties:** 15% sauvignon, 80% sémillon, 5% muscadelle. **Production:** *13 tonneaux,* 10,000 bottles CB. **Direct sales and by mail order:** in France and abroad. Monsieur Ferbos, La Garenne, Preignac, 33210 Langon. Tel. 56 63 27 22.

Quantity or quality? This is the overriding and omnipresent problem of Sauternes right down to the choice of harvesters. For Jean-Pierre Ferbos there is not a moment's hesitation: "It is better to have five or six people who know the job than a larger team who know nothing." Coming from a family of wine brokers and buyers for four generations, the proprietor of La Garenne looks back with satisfaction over twenty-five years of careful vinification. He insists on looking after everything personally: "Cultivation, vinification, bottling and marketing are all in my hands." You can rely on them.

La Gauche (Domaine de) ♙ ♙ ♙ ♙ ♙

Commune: Bommes. **Proprietor:** Jean Baro. **Size of vineyard:** 2.3 hectares. **Average age of vines:** 30 years. **Varieties:** 20% sauvignon, 60% sémillon, 20% muscadelle. **Production:** *6 tonneaux,* 7,200 bottles C B. **Visits:** by appointment. Jean Baro, tel. 56 63 60 76. **Direct sales and by mail order:** in France. M. Baro, Domaine de la Gauche, Bommes, 33210 Langon.

Until 1980 this *cru* used to be called "Domaine de la Gueritte" (the sentry-box). Jean Baro stood sentinel, hoping that the rosy light of a socialist dawn would soon colour the sky of France and Sauternes. His hopes came true in 1981. To mark the event in his own manner, he gave his label the new name of "Domaine de la Gauche" ("gauche" meaning "left") and replaced the shield crowned with a mediaeval helmet with the rose in hand. Marking the passing of history in this way has proved profitable. The party faithful set their hearts on backing Jean Baro's initiative and he has found clients and friends from Marseilles to Tourcoing and from Hendaye to Strasburg. "I have a lot of clients who are all in agreement on the

Jean Baro swears he has his heart on the left and that he makes good wine.

quality of the goods," he says, for this experienced lifelong grower is also a capable salesman. Apart from the *cru*'s unusual name, I also like the words on the label: *Vin blanc unique au monde*. I think that his "crème de tête" is worthy of the highest praise.

La Gueritte (Domaine de) ⚥ → La Gauche

Lamothe (Château)

2e cru classé

Commune: Sauternes. **Proprietors:** M. and Madame Jean Despujols. Consultant oenologist: M. Bouyx. **Size of vineyard:** 8 hectares. **Average age of vines:** 30 to 35 years. **Varieties:** 70% sauvignon, 15% sémillon, 15% muscadelle. **Production:** 22,000 bottles CB. **Visits:** from 9 a.m. to noon and 2 to 6 p.m. Tel. 56 63 61 22. **Direct sales and by mail order:** in France and abroad. Château Lamothe, Sauternes, 33210 Langon. **Retail sales:** through Bordeaux and for export.

Between Filhot and La Tour Blanche, this vineyard lies about 500 metres from the village of Sauternes. On the western spur of the hill, in the Gallo-Roman period, there stood a small fort of which traces can still be seen today. According to archaeologists, it was a garrison for newly arrived troops. This has nothing to do however with the name of the *cru* – Château Lamothe d'Assault – at the beginning of the nineteenth century. In 1814 it belonged to the English merchant, Jacques Dowling. Later, it was divided up (see Lamothe Guignard). Before coming into the hands of the Despujols in 1961, it belonged to the Dezeimeries de La Porte, Massieux, Dudébat, Bergey and Bastit Saint-Martin families. Every fresh transaction almost invariably resulted in a web of complications: family trusts, lawsuits and so on.

The Despujols are experienced growers who run their estate in the most traditional way. Without ever claiming to be sublime, their wines are finely balanced and offer good value for money. The '86 is ready to drink and its full-bodied character will be appreciated. The 88 is naturally riding on the crest of the tidal wave set in motion by the best botrytis imaginable. As for the 89, the Despujols are convinced that the year of bicentenary of the French Revolution will be for them the "year of the century".

Lamothe Guignard (Château)

2e cru classé

Commune: Sauternes. **Proprietors:** Philippe and Jacques Guignard. **Size of vineyard:** 15 hectares. **Average age of vines:** 30 years. **Varieties:** 5% sauvignon, 90% sémillon, 5% muscadelle. **Production:** 25 *tonneaux*, 25,000 bottles CB. **Visits:** by appointment only. Monsieur Guignard, tel. 56 63 60 28. **Direct sales and by mail order:** in France exclusively. Philippe or Jacques Guignard, Château Lamothe, Sauternes, 33210 Langon. **Retail sales:** through the Bordeaux trade.

Though neighbours, the two Lamothes greatly differ, say the owners.

This estate has its peak on one of the highest clayey/gravelly hillocks in the commune of Sauternes. In 1814 it was known by the name of Lamothe d'Assault and belonged to Jean-François de Borie, who sold it to Jacques Dowling. As a result of family conflicts, the property was split up into several parts. Towards the end of the last century the largest fell to Charles Joseph Bergey, who handed it on to his daughter Marie Angèle Tissot. Then in 1958, Armand Bastit Saint-Martin came to preside over the fate of the *cru*. He was the president of the department's Caisse de Crédit Agricole before Pierre Perromat. On his death in 1980, Philippe and Jacques Guignard acquired the estate. Since then, they have devoted much care and attention to developing this fine vineyard. The 1981 vintage was their first harvest: a beautiful, brilliant straw colour, a fine nose of crystallised pineapple, apricot and honey; a wine with great stamina, very long in the mouth, clean, rich, whose bouquet has an astonishing persistence with a clearly marked musky character and a slightly spicy finish. Its price is relatively modest; but Lamothe is an up-and-coming wine.

Lamourette (Château)   ♀ ♀ ♀ ♀ ♀

Commune: Bommes. **Proprietors:** Paul Léglise & Fille. Consultant oenologist: Albert Bouyx. **Size of vineyard:** 7.4 hectares. **Average age of vines:** 30 years. **Varieties:** 6% sauvignon, 86% sémillon, 8% muscadelle. **Production:** 19 *tonneaux*, 6,000 bottles CB. **Visits:** preferably by appointment. Anne-Marie Léglise, tel. 56 63 63 58. **Direct sales and by mail order:** in France and abroad. Monsieur Paul Léglise, Château Lamourette, Bommes, 33210 Langon.

Millet's spirit lives on - "L'Angélus" at Lamourette.

This very name conjures up a whole host of images. Even before tasting the wine, it inspires feelings of tenderness. A diminutive of *amour* it means "fleeting love". The feminity of the name is highly appropriate, since the vineyard of Lamourette has been handed down from mother to daughter since 1860. Anne-Marie Léglise continues this line today. The wine is pale and floral, very Barsac in style: perfect for dinner on Mother's Day or for putting colour into the cheeks of a shy fiancée.

Lange (Château) ♀♀♀♀♀

Commune: Bommes. **Proprietors:** Robert Picot & Fils. Director: Daniel Picot. **Size of vineyard:** 15 hectares. **Average age of vines:** 25 years. **Varieties:** 20% sauvignon, 70% sémillon, 10% muscadelle. **Production:** 35,000 bottles CB. **Visits:** Robert or Daniel Picot, tel. 56 63 13 60. **Direct sales and by mail order:** abroad. Château Lange, Bommes, 33210 Langon. **Retail sales:** in bulk delivered to the merchants at the time of bottling: Ets Germain in Berson; Union blanquefortaise, suppliers to the French Navy.

Now retired, Robert Picot has delegated his talent for making good wine to his son Daniel. He comes from Barsac and is owner of the estate through his wife, who is from Preignac. Rigorously conservative, both father and son refuse to produce dry wines and sweet wines simultaneously. "We are traditionalists. You cannot produce quality by asking the vines to meet all needs." Having the advantage of very varied terrains for which long experience has taught them the best choice of varieties, the Picots are producers of excellent Sauternes. I like their wine and the way they make it. Nor am I alone, for they won a gold medal in Paris in 1978 and another in Bordeaux in 1980. The wine of Château Lange is a perfect example of a classic Sauternes of constant quality. It bears comparison with *crus* of more distinguished reputation, or even with certain *crus classés*.

Lapinesse (Château)

Commune: Barsac. **Proprietor:** Henri Guinabert. Château Villefranche, Barsac, 33720 Podensac. Tel. 56 27 16 39. Consultant oenologist: Pierre Sudraud. **Size of vineyard:** 4.13 hectares. **Average age of vines:** 30 years. **Varieties:** 10% sauvignon, 85% sémillon, 5% muscadelle. **Production:** 12 *tonneaux.* **Retail sales:** in bulk.

sold in bulk

Monsieur Guinabert recently bought this established and pretty little vineyard from M. Jean Danglade. His first harvest was in 1986 and, in view of the short time-scale, the results are highly encouraging. He still has a great deal to do to organize things as he wishes, for he plans to create a label and to bottle at the château.

Lardit (Clos)

Commune: Barsac. **Proprietor:** Georges Danglade. Consultant oenologist: Jacoby Laboratory in Podensac. **Size of vineyard:** 4.3 hectares. **Average age of vines:** 25 years. **Varieties:** 20% sauvignon, 70% sémillon, 10% muscadelle. **Production:** 10 *tonneaux,* 6,000 bottles CB. **Direct sales and by mail order:** in France. Georges Danglade, Lardit, Barsac, 33720 Podensac. Tel. 56 27 17 85.

Modestly, Georges Danglade, the mayor of Barsac, has decided not to allow himself to be tempted by delusions of grandeur. Lardit is not a château, but a "clos", and will remain so. This little vineyard to the care of which, handed down to him by his paternal grandfather, he has added several other plots is extremely dear to his heart. If you ask him to tell you what his wine is like he replies, "typical of the Barsac appellation". Georges Danglade is similar in character to Clos Lardit, genuine and charming, with the *terroir* in his blood. You can always try to buy a few bottles from him, but as he has a great many friends needing regular supplies, you would do better, if you want to taste it, to contrive an invitation to the party given in honour of local notables after the next municipal elections.

Laribotte (Château)

Commune: Preignac. **Proprietor:** Jean Lahiteau. Consultant oenologist: Jean-Paul Pauquet. **Size of vineyard:** 11.5 hectares. **Average age of vines:** 20 years. **Varieties:** 15% sauvignon, 80% sémillon, 5% muscadelle. **Production:** 30 *tonneaux* 35,000 bottles CB. **Visits:** by appointment only. Monsieur Lahiteau, tel. 56 63 27 88. **Direct sales and by mail order:** in France. Château Laribotte, quartier de Sauches, Preignac, 33210 Langon. **Retail sales:** through the firm of Lichine.

"From father to son since 1855", are the words to be read on the label of this *cru*. Is it by chance that the date coincides with that of the famous classification? By no means: it was chosen deliberately by proprietors who must have thought that if they used the date 1789 they might start a revolution. For it is really since the first abolition of the French monarchy that the Lahiteaus have been growers in Preignac from father to son. Moreover, the name *La Hitau* apparently does have republican connotations though no one has explained to me exactly what they are, from the time when the *sans-culottes* began to cultivate the nobles' vines for themselves. In *L'Amateur de Bordeaux* I have already had occasion to praise the quality of Laribotte, especially the '82, with its bouquet of fern and linden, rather spicy with hints of muscadelle and botrytis. Interesting.

L'Arieste (Château) ♙ → Voigny

Larose-Monteils (Château) ♚ ♚ ♚ ♚ ♚

Commune: Preignac. **Proprietor:** Georges Cambefort. Directors, estate and vineyard managers: Georges Cambefort and his son. Consultant oenologist: Albert Bouyx. **Size of vineyard:** 9 hectares. **Average age of vines:** 35 to 40 years. **Varieties:** 10% sauvignon, 80% sémillon, 10% muscadelle. **Production:** 25 *tonneaux*. **Direct sales and by mail order:** in France. Georges Cambefort, Château Larose-Monteils, Preignac, 33210 Langon. Tel. 56 63 24 63. **Retail sales.**

Following its first appearance at the beginning of the century, Domaine de Monteil rapidly acquired a reputation with the négociants of Bordeaux and with a small circle of private clients. But as Monteil was also the name of a place in Preignac, much confusion arose with similar-sounding neighbouring *crus*. This is the reason why, thirty years later, Georges Cambefort created the official and unique name "Larose-Monteils". Depending on the vintage, he and his son decide on the quantity of wine to be sold in bulk to the trade and that to be château-bottled. You may be sure that they select with the greatest care the wine destined to bear the château label. The honour of seven generations of proprietors-growers is at stake. With the passage of time the size of the vineyard has hardly altered, laid out in large plots on excellent gravelly soil. The part that lies in Haut-Preignac consists of gravel 30 cm thick laid over a subsoil of blue clay: perfect, in short. Georges Cambefort's wines tend towards delicacy and finesse, in the Barsac style. The 1982 vintage seems outstandingly successful. It is a wine to be bought and tasted with your eyes closed, in absolute confidence, if any can be found today. You would be well advised to reserve some '88 but you may already be too late.

Monsieur Cambefort's diploma.

La Tour Blanche (Château)

1er cru classé

Commune: Bommes. **Proprietor:** The Ministry of Agriculture. Manager: Jean-Pierre Jausserand. **Size of vineyard:** 27 hectares. **Average age of vines:** 40 years. **Varieties:** 19% sauvignon, 78% sémillon, 3% muscadelle. **Production:** 55,000 bottles CB. **Visits:** Monday to Friday from 9 a.m. to noon and 2 to 5 p.m. **Direct sales and by mail order:** in France. Château La Tour Blanche, Bommes, 33210 Langon. Tel. 56 63 61 55. **Retail sales:** through Bordeaux and in Belgium and America.

It would be easy to assume that this name derived quite naturally from a tower on the estate or attached to the château, its white stonework silhouetted against the surrounding green of the countryside. Such an idea would be supported by the *cru*'s label, which depicts a squat little tower of white stone. But such is not the case. The name takes its origins from Jean Saint-Marc de Latourblanche, Louis XVI's chief treasurer, who died in Bommes on October 20, 1784.

In 1855 La Tour Blanche was classed as a *Premier Cru* and the records of the Bordeaux Chamber of Commerce place it at the top of the category, just after Yquem. It belonged at that time to a rich merchant called Focke, who died shortly afterwards. His widow sold the estate to Merman, Capdeville and Maître who resold it to Daniel Osiris, a financier as enterprising as he was original. He was also a patron of the arts who liked to "spread happiness" around him. He died in 1907. His will, drawn up a year earlier, contained an unusual codicil: "I give and bequeath to the French State my property situated in the commune of Bommes near Sauternes, called Château La Tour Blanche, with all its easements, outbuildings and

The cru *does not take its name from the white dove-cote.*

vineyards."A special clause stipulated that this bequest would be fulfilled on condition that the Ministry of Agriculture set up an agricultural college on the estate which would guarantee "free practical instruction for the people". This wish was realized in 1911.

Since that time, Château La Tour Blanche has been devoted to the training of generations of aspiring viticulturalists. Students take part in every aspect of the work, both on the vines and in the vat-house and cellar. The governing body consists of well-known people from the region. The wine is not now one of the appellation's stars, but it still has a good and reliable reputation.

Latrezotte (Château)   ♈ ♈ ♈ ♈ ♈

Commune: Barsac. **Proprietor:** Mlle Marie-Pierre Badourès. Vineyard manager: M. Glock. Consultant oenologist: M. Rolland. **Size of vineyard:** 10 hectares. **Average age of vines:** 40 years. **Varieties:** 15% sauvignon, 70% sémillon, 15% muscadelle. **Production:** 20 to 35 *tonneaux*, 10,000 bottles CB. **Visits:** weekdays, by appointment. Tel 56 27 16 50. **Direct sales and by mail order:** Château Latrezotte, Barsac, 33720 Podensac. **Retail sales:** Maison Daniel Querre, Place Guadet, 33500 Libourne.

"They must be tall and handsome with blue eyes." Mademoiselle Marie-Pierre Badourès selects her harvesters like thoroughbreds. "I am very fond of my harvesters", she adds with conviction, "but I tolerate neither sloth nor familiarity." This extract from a report by Lucien Bourdelles, published in the *Sud-Ouest* newspaper on November 11, 1985, illustrates one aspect of the personality of "the good fairy of Latrezotte". She is committed body and soul to her property, which stands proudly on the plateau of la Pinesse to the far south of the commune. "I have always loved the house, its furniture and ancient trees; I was obliged to take on the estate as well as a result of family circumstances." Meticulous, energetic and fervently enthusiastic, Marie-Pierre Badourès's passion is infectious. For her, Latrezotte is an oasis of good living. It is an enchanted land, too, with its bamboo forest, large enough to make you think you are in Asia, and its peach tree growing out of the stones. An island of peace, where an ecological approach is neither an academic philosophy nor a political programme, but a way of life. The proprietor is possessive, too: she runs her estate entirely by herself and she loves it dearly. "In harvesting grape by grape, according to our traditional methods, I get to know every single vine."

The firm of Daniel Querre in Libourne has sole distribution rights. But each year is sold separately, vintage by vintage. No over-tasty decisions are taken, however. The wines which are put on to the market have been allowed to reach the point at which they are ready to drink. When the 79 was finished (a very fine wine, in truth) it was followed by the '81, which was very successful. Let no more be said of the '80; it was unsatisfactory and sold off in bulk. I should like to point out in passing that this practice, while it protects the reputation of the Château's label, greatly lowers the quality of the Sauternes bottled by the trade. The '85 is now on the market and has been reserved in advance by several connoisseurs. My advice is to reserve a few cases of '86 without delay. Mademoiselle Badourès could give lessons in marketing to many of the young students coming out business school. For the lover of truth, sensitivity and good Barsac wine, Latrezotte is outstanding. That is why I have given it five glasses, of which one is full of affection.

Laville (Château)

Commune: Preignac. **Proprietors:** Mesdames Barbe and Maillé. Consultant oenologist: Pierre Sudraud. **Size of vineyard:** 18 hectares. **Average age of vines:** 25 years. **Varieties:** 15% sauvignon, 80% sémillon, 5% muscadelle. **Production:** 40 *tonneaux*, 12,000 bottles CB. **Visits:** Monday to Friday from 8 a.m. to noon and 2 to 6 p.m. Saturdays and Sundays by prior appointment. Tel. 56 63 28 14 or 56 63 18 14. **Direct sales and by mail order:** in France and abroad. Mesdames Barbe and Maillé, Château Laville, Preignac, 33210 Langon. **Retail sales:** two thirds of the production is sold in bulk.

Surrounding its château, the estate forms a huge enclosure of 22 hectares of which 18 are presently under vine. It is one of the oldest *crus* in the commune of Preignac, listed by Charles Cocks in 1850 and classed in successive editions of *Bordeaux et ses Vins* among the *bourgeois supérieurs*. In the middle of the last century, it belonged to a banker from Langon called Alary. Then it came into the hands of a wholesale grocer from Preignac called Laroumet, who bought the property in several stages, finishing with the château in 1895. Laroumet pioneered the selling of bottled wine when the majority of his neighbours were selling only in the *barrique*. After his death in 1920, his heirs could only dissolve the family trust by putting the estate up for public auction. The successful bidder was P. Despujols, a proprietor at Sainte-Croix-du-Mont, who eagerly crossed the river to take possession and extend the vineyard. It was in 1960 that Jean Delmond, returned to France and having lost his possessions in Algeria, when that country gained its independance, set his heart on Château Laville. His period of ownership brough Laville entirely justified acclaim. Since 1971 his two daughters, Mesdames Barbe and Maillé, have given their closest attention to running the estate.

Le Dauphin de Lalague → Guiraud

L'Ermitage (Château) → Partarrieu

Les Justices (Château)

Commune: Preignac. **Proprietor:** Christian Médeville. **Size of vineyard:** 8.5 hectares. **Average age of vines:** 25 years. **Varieties:** 12% sauvignon, 84% sémillon, 4% muscadelle. **Production:** 22 *tonneaux*, 20,000 bottles CB. **Visits:** weekdays from 9 a.m. to 6 p.m. Tel. 56 63 27 59. **Direct sales and by mail order:** in France and abroad. C. Médeville, Preignac, 33210 Langon. **Retail sales:** a small amount abroad.

For over two centuries this has been the ancestral property of the Médevilles in Preignac. Following René, Joseph and Numa, the father, grandfather and great-grandfather respectively of the present owner, Christian Médeville maintains a continuing tradition of quality. His other *cru*, Château Gilette (see above), is pledged to providing venerable wines. Les Justices furnishes younger wines which are not less than two or three years old when they are bottled. Here are some of the most remarkable among them:

1988: Elegant light yellow colour, intense, complex nose, evident botrytis. Aromas of great finesse, gingerbread, orange, fig, hazelnut. Lively and elegant, full, round and rich. Harmonious and concentrated wine, very well balanced.

1986: Brilliant golden yellow. An intense, complex, fresh (mint) nose. Hints of crystallized apricot and orange, aromas of toast and spices. Rich, powerful, unctuous and lingering. A harmonious wine, flattering to nose and mouth; well botrytized.

1985: Very elegant buttercup-yellow colour, a floral bouquet of great distinction, round with wonderful savours of crystallized orange, hints of toast and spices blending perfectly with fine woody notes. A wonderful sensation of freshness and balance.

1983: A beautiful topaz colour. A bouquet of rare complexity blending pear, beeswax, cinnamon, with a hint of vanilla and liquorice, a pinch of cocoa.

1981: Bright pale yellow colour. Flattering to the nose with aromas of caramel, vanilla, apricot; intense sweetness. Unctuous and agreeable to the palate.

1976: A lovely colour, slightly golden. Exquisite hints of honey and flowers. Astonishing balance; the roundness of the texture and subtlety of nuances accompany the sweetness of a liquor rich in untransformed sugar. Long in the mouth.

1970: Deep hue. An ample nose marked by the presence of muscadelle. Classical aromas of honey and apricot with a nuance of the choicest tea. Full and subtle, the finish is superb. Fantastically long in the mouth, up to a minute.

1961: A golden colour of rare limpidity and vivacity. An admirably complex bouquet of citrus fruit preserves. Exceptional density and richness. Incomparable.

Well done, Les Justices!

Les Rochers (Château) ♟ → Voigny

L'Estrémade (Domaine de) ♟ → Rabaud-Promis

Liot (Château) ♟♟♟♟♟

Commune: Barsac. **Proprietor:** Joseph David. Consultant oenologist: M. Llorca. **Size of vineyard:** 21 hectares. **Varieties:** 15% sauvignon, 80% sémillon, 5% muscadelle. **Production:** 55 *tonneaux*, 50,000 bottles CB. Visits: by appointment. Tel. 56 27 15 31. **Direct sales and by mail order:** in France. Monsieur Daniels, Château Liot, Barsac, 33720 Podensac. **Retail sales.**

Liot is a very old Barsac hamlet to the south of Château Climens. This Gascon word means a sort of sledge used in forestry. Its etymological root is *leye*, which has given the French words "laie" or "layon" meaning a forest track. I believe that at one time wood from deeper in the forests was sent to the Ciron through Liot. Attention having been duly paid to etymology, I shall now simply add that Château Liot is among the best Barsac *bourgeois* wines. Grape varieties are entirely traditional with precisely the right proportion of sauvignon and muscadelle to give vigour and bite to the unctuousness of the sémillon. Joseph David bottles only the good vintages.

The rest is sold in bulk to the trade. It should be mentioned that this *cru* from Barsac is officially declared in the Sauternes appellation. I have nothing against this practice, but I think it is nevertheless a pity for the growers of Barsac.

Malle (Château de)

2e cru classé

Commune: Preignac. **Proprietor:** The Comtesse de Bournazel. Cellar master: M. Pivonet. Consultant oenologist: Pierre Sudraud. **Size of vineyard:** 27 hectares. **Varieties:** 22% sauvignon, 75% sémillon, 3% muscadelle. **Production:** 150 *tonneaux*. **Visits:** Mlle Lucchesi, tel. 56 63 28 67. **Direct sales and by mail order:** in France. Château de Malle, Preignac, 33210 Langon. **Retail sales.**

Long before they became lords of Yquem, the Lur Saluces were masters of Malle. Eutrope-Alexandre de Lur Saluces, the Comte d'Uza, married Jeanne de Malle in 1702. She came from a Preignac family with origins going back some five hundred years. At the very beginning of the seventeenth century Jacques de Malle, the president of the Parlement in Bordeaux, built the beautiful château which we can still admire today. It is a little masterpiece of French classicism in the style of François

The grounds of Malle seem to have been designed on a Florentine model.

141

Officially classified as a historic monument, Château de Malle...

Mansart, while the grounds seem to have been designed on a Florentine model: a theatre in stone containing sculpted figures inspired by the *commedia dell'arte*. A long and lofty terrace offers a magnificent panorama over the Sauternes vineyards. The overall effect is majestic but retains a certain intimacy. The château and the gardens are officially classified as national historic monuments. The mistress of the house is the Comtesse de Bournazel, whose husband Pierre de Bournazel (who sadly died in the prime of life) was a direct descendant of the Lur Saluces. Pierre de Bournazel, a qualified oenologist, left his mark on Bordeaux viticulture. He was admired for his extreme courtesy which was never in the slightest degree condescending. I remember him as a gentleman in every sense of the term. Within the château, his wife preserves the dignity and quality it has always known: furniture, pictures and ornaments have a timeless air with, as she likes to say of her wine, "a capti-

is one of the most elegant in the département.

vating scent of history through the crystal". Speaking of its older cousin, Château d'Yquem, a nineteenth-century poet and gourmed exclaimed: "L'extravagance du parfait"! Malle on the other hand might be described as the epitomy of classicism, of less ample body but with more delicacy, with less masculine assertion and more feminine discretion. Indeed the great Sauternes may be attributed a sex.

The breeding and distinction – in short the true nobility – of the place are also clearly evident in the wine of the *cru*. It is not so much its power which is its principal characteristic, but an aromatic finesse in which honey and almonds are in counterpoint, rather like a duet for flute and harp. All the recent vintages of Malle present this inimitable quality, common to all very great Sauternes, without being either too thick or too heavy. They are seductive wines *par excellence*. Alongside the production of sweet white wines, Château de Malle also has a vineyard for red wines. 143

The reason for this is that the estate's land extends right up to the Graves appellation. Under the name of "Château de Cardaillan", the wine lover can find agreeable wines distinguished by their fruit and freshness, and which have the advantage of being reasonably priced.

Mauras (Château)   ♟ ♟ ♟ ♟ ♟

Commune: Bommes. **Proprietor:** Société civile de la Rive Gauche. Managed by: Société Viticole de France. Director: Jean-Luc Dualé. Vineyard manager: Michel Beaulac. Cellar master and consultant oenologist: Jean-Pierre Kauffer. **Size of vineyard:** 15 hectares. **Average age of vines:** 20 years. **Varieties:** 30% sauvignon, 65% sémillon, 5% muscadelle. **Production:** 40 *tonneaux*, 45,000 bottles CB. **Visits:** by appointment only. Monsieur Michel Beaulac, tel. 56 63 61 59. **Direct sales:** Château Mauras, Bommes, 33210 Langon (no sales by mail order). **Retail sales:** through the Bordeaux trade.

This attractive property used to belong to my dear old friend André Abadie, who until his death lived in the Château de Carignan in the appellation of Premières Côtes de Bordeaux. However, he always took particular pleasure in serving his distinguished guests (his table was one of the most select in the *département*) a glass of Mauras with their dessert. Despite the great difference in our ages, we were very close. He had a keen mind and discreetly wielded considerable influence. A widower with two daughters as his heirs, he wanted to prepare the succession in the best possible way. To help him, I agreed to look after the sale of Château Mauras, which came about in 1973. The sale was clinched with a double telephone conversation. In one ear I had André Abadie and in the other David Bennett, representing a

Mauras, an attractive property - both pleasure and profit are found here.

group of foreign investors. It lasted about half an hour. When I hung up the two telephones, Mauras was sold. The Société Viticole de France later extended its interests by buying other estates in the Bordeaux area as well as in Italy and Spain (it then changed its name to the Société Viticole Européenne). Men who are pure and simple financiers tend not to make long-term vignerons. The vineyards abroad were sold off, whereas since December 1986 Jean-Luc Dualé, a director of the firm, has managed to become owner of other Bordeaux *crus* apart from Mauras, namely Château Grava in Haux and Château Vieira in La Sauve. He also rents Château Mauvesin in Moulis.

Mauras's terroir is classic, with layers of sand and clay over a bed of limestone. The vines are required to give the highest yield in the appellation, but the oenological skills of Jean-Pierre Kauffer yield us wines which are young and fresh in style, and which I rank among the better modern Sauternes.

Mayne (Château du) ♀♀♀♀♀

Commune: Barsac. **Proprietor:** S.C.I. Château Haut-Bailly Le Mayne. **Manager:** Jean Sanders. Consultant oenologist: Pierre Sudraud. **Size of vineyard:** 8 hectares. **Average age of vines:** 40 years. **Varieties:** 20% sauvignon, 80% sémillon. **Production:** 17 *tonneaux*, 20,400 bottles CB. **Visits:** daily. Madame Tauzin, tel. 56 27 16 07. **Direct sales and by mail order:** in France. M. Sanders, Barsac, 33720 Podensac. **Retail sales**.

The Sanders family have owned this property for over half a century. Daniel Sanders acquired it in 1937 after coveting it for many years, for it took him back to his ancestral roots. Situated between the railway and Château Suau, it benefits from a particularly warm microclimate favouring early ripening. With its gravel and thick sand over a relatively deep aquifer, the nature of the soil tends to be more like the

terrain of Sauternes than Barsac. Though influenced by these geological factors, the wine remains fine and delicate and never shows the slightest sign of heaviness. It is rather in the style of the dwelling which fills the place of a château: distinguished, well-to-do, rather stylish, with a sort of discreet charm. The visitor will always be warmly welcomed and can buy bottles at reasonable prices. The recent vintages were successful, especially '83, powerful and distinguished, which can be drunk now although it shows every sign of being suitable for ageing.

Menate (Château) ♀ → *Ménota*

Ménota (Château)

Y Y Y Y Y

Commune: Barsac. **Proprietor:** S.C.E.A. du Château Ménota. Directors: Monsieur and Madame Noël Labat. Consultant oenologist: Frédéric Labat. **Size of vineyard:** 29 hectares. **Varieties:** 50% sauvignon, 50% sémillon. **Production:** *80 tonneaux,* 80,000 bottles CB. **Visits**: by appointment. Tel. 56 27 15 80. **Direct sales and by mail order:** in France and abroad. Château Ménota, Barsac, 33720 Podensac.

Magistrates, starting with the presidents of the Parlement in Bordeaux, have always been part-time viticulturalists. François de Pignéguy was not the most celebrated among them, but we know that in the sixteenth century he presided over both the Parlement and the destiny of Château Ménota. This magnificent fortified manorhouse, which looks as if might have come straight out of the pages of a children's fairy story, would indeed make the perfect setting for tales of the chivalrous deeds of knights in shining armour. Covering twenty-nine hectares, the vineyard is planted with equal proportions of sauvignon and sémillon. Such a balance is rare, if not unique, in Barsac. It gives the wine a sturdy structure and makes it suitable for long ageing. All things being relative, a hint of rather biting dryness can be detected which is in contrast with the excessive sweetness to be found in certain neighbouring Sauternes. Ménota is a *cru* which has as much character as its owner, Noël Labat. The *Guide Hachette des vins de France* attributes its originality to "the smell of a freshly plucked chicken". (A further edition will perhaps specify the breed of the chicken). I must confess that such an idea had not occurred to me. The Ménota '81, which won a gold medal at the Paris Agricultural Competition, is superbly fat and rich: a fine capon among wines.

Ménota too bears the mark of Sauternes' warlike history.

Monteils (Domaine de)

♟♟♟♟♟

Commune: Preignac. **Proprietor:** Jean-Claude Cousin. **Size of vineyard:** 8 hectares. **Average age of vines:** 45 years. **Varieties:** 5% sauvignon, 90% sémillon, 5% muscadelle. **Production:** 22 *tonneaux*, a small proportion put in bottle. **Visits:** by appointment only. Monsieur Cousin, tel. 56 63 28 87. **Direct sales and by mail order:** in France and abroad. Jean-Claude Cousin, Médudon, Preignac, 33210 Langon. **Retail sales:** in bulk.

The estate is situated on either side of the road to Villandraut, between the railway, the motorway, the valley of the Ciron and Château de Malle. Monteils is a very old locality in the commune of Preignac: still small, at one time it was no bigger than a hamlet. Jean-Claude Cousin's ancestors have lived at Médudon, immediately to the north-east of Monteils, since 1867. The soil here is gravelly and sandy. Making an appointment with the proprietor to taste his excellent wine on the spot is recommended.

Mont-Joye (Château)

♟♟♟♟♟

Commune: Barsac. **Proprietor:** Franck Glaunès. Consultant oenologist: Albert Bouyx and the Soussac Laboratory. **Size of vineyard:** 20 hectares. **Average age of vines:** 35 years. **Varieties:** 30% sauvignon, 60% sémillon, 10% muscadelle. **Production:** 40,000 bottles CB. **Visits:** by appointment. Tel. 56 71 12 73. **Direct sales and by mail order:** in France. Franck Glaunès, Domaine du Pas, Saint-Georges, 33190 Casseuil. **Retail sales:** in bulk and for export.

The name Mont-Joye, or Montjoie, means a small mound, generally of stone, at the side of the road, often at a crossroads. Frequently surmounted by an ornamental symbol or a cross, these were originally shrines or offerings to God and itinerant knights invoking their protection for the surrounding country. Then these mounds became monuments commemorating battles. During the Hundred Years War, the famous battle cry "Montjoie Saint-Denis!" came to mean something like "Saint-Denis be with us!" During the Renaissance, "montjoie" was also used to mean the banner at the head of an army.

All this goes to prove how old the locality is. Truth to tell, the stones still exist here and there but are now mostly used to make walls round the vineyards. As the name of a wine, Mont-Joye appeared towards the end of the last century, and its growth is largely due to Dr Despujols, grandfather of the present owner, Franck Glaunès. A highly colourful character, the doctor, who was for a long time the president of the Federation of the Barsac AOC and founder of the Sauternes' Viticultural Office, is still famous in the Bordeaux region, at least as much for his system of "cutting back the new young vine shoots" as for his therapeutic treatments. On his death his daughter took over running the estate. It was she who restored the vineyard after the 1956 frosts.

Situated to the west of the commune, the terroir is for the most part made up of red clay-chalk soil with a few spots of more or less dense sand on a bed of asteroidian limestone. The relatively high proportion of sauvignon should be noted – the same is also true of muscadelle – compared with the traditional balance of varieties in Barsac. This gives the wine of Château Mont-Joye's wine greater alcoholic strength and thus reduces its sweetness. People who like bite and are not over-keen on sugar can therefore give their palate a treat.

Myrat (Château)

2e cru classé

In 1975 Max de Pontac tore up his vines, despairing of any rise in the price of Sauternes. His timing was appalling, since prices immediately started to go up. On his death in 1988 his two sons immediately began to replant, just in time to save it from losing the right to the appellations. Our next edition should celebrate the renaissance of a great wine. (Editor's note).

Nairac (Château)

Y Y Y Y Y

2e cru classé

Commune: Barsac. **Proprietor:** Nicole Tari. Vineyard manager: Guy Lassauvageux. Consultant oenologists: Messrs. Sudraud and Bouyx. **Size of vineyard:** 16 hectares. **Average age of vines:** 30 years. **Varieties:** 6% sauvignon, 90% sémillon, 4% muscadelle. **Production:** 24,000 to 25,000 bottles CB. **Visits:** Nicole Tari (tel. 56 88 34 02). **Direct sales and by mail order:** in France and abroad. Château Nairac, Barsac, 33720 Podensac. **Retail sales:** through Bordeaux.

Since the day the *seigneur* of Luzies presented the Duc d'Epernon with spurs of finely-wrought silver, liquid gold has flowed in the crystal glasses of Nairac. This château bears the name of a very famous family of Bordeaux négociants, a powerful Protestant family which left its mark on Bordeaux's economy in the eighteenth century and had financial links with such distinguished firms as Rabaud, Clamageran, Balguerie, Brown (see Cantenac-Brown in the volume on Margaux), Exshaw, Guestier and so on. The most famous was Paul Nairac, who was not only a merchant but also a shipowner. His largest vessel, *L'Imposant*, was of 900 tons, that is, forty-five times the present weight of the harvests of Nairac!

The family's town house stood at the end of the Cours de Verdun in Bordeaux. Built to plans by Victor Louis, it is today the administrative headquarters of the Société Bordelaise de Crédit Industriel et Commercial, an old finance house of the Chartrons. It is certain that Victor Louis also had a hand in the preliminary designs for Château Nairac in Barsac, as the posthumous discovery of the first outlines of the elegant residence in his sketch-books goes to prove. But the final shape of the building and the plans are the work of the architect Mollié, who at the same time, in 1786, was also designing the panelling for the choir in the church at Barsac (Ph. Maffre and J.-P. Bériac: *Bordeaux néoclassique*). The château was built on the site of an aristocratic dwelling whose history is not known. The style of the façade is in the pure Victor Louis school: on the ground floor, this can be seen

Neither grandiose nor monumental, but classical and superb: Château Nairac.

in, windows with semicircular arches set in rectangular niches cut into the wall, ornamental balustrades below the windows and above the central portion of the building, decorative motifs on the internal fireplaces, and so on. As is demonstrated by some of the preliminary architectural drawings, some parts of the building are the joint work of André Mollié and Elisée Nairac, Paul's brother and partner. Thus Château Nairac belongs to a collection of the finest summer dwellings in Gironde, inspired by Victor Louis.

It stands at the entrance to the Barsac appellation as you approach from Bordeaux on the R.N. 113, on the right just before the village. One part of the vineyard starts at the foot of the château walls and stretches right into the village. Another part consists of excellent plots on the plateau called "Haut-Barsac", not far from Château Climens. Tom Heeter, who comes from a family of Ohio industrialists, fell in love almost simultaneously with the great wines of Barsac and Nicole Tari, the daughter of Nicolas and sister of Pierre of Château Giscours at Margaux. In the time that they were together they restored Nairac's lustre and its fame, and also produced three children, of whom the eldest is Nicolas. In view of the work that has been undertaken and the investment of time and energy that has been made in this estate, it seems to me both right and desirable that in a few years Nicolas Heeter should be master of Nairac.

Château Nairac can attain the very heights of finesse. And when the quality is not right, the wine is not sold under the name of the château. The 1977, 1978 and 1984 vintages were all declassified. Each harvest ferments and matures in new wood; an unheard-of luxury which even the greatest do not always dare to indulge in. For ten years Nairac has been making superbly sumptuous wines. Nairac is to Barsac as Verlaine is to French poetry.

Ormes (Château des) 🜨 → *Armajan des Ormes*

Padouën (Château)

Commune: Barsac. **Proprietors:** M. and Madame Michel Canot. Consultant oenologist: Pierre Sudraud. **Size of vineyard:** 10 hectares. **Average age of vines:** 30 years. **Varieties:** 15% sauvignon, 70% sémillon, 15% muscadelle. **Production:** 28 *tonneaux*. **Direct sales:** Château Padouën, Barsac 33720 Podensac. Tel. 56 27 07 28. **Retail sales:** through Bordeaux.

Château Padouën has belonged to the Canots since 1984. They are traditionalists: their methods of cultivation and vinification are the "old-fashioned" ones and they still sell their harvest in bulk to the Bordeaux trade. It is certain that they are going to do more château-bottling but the decision will not take effect overnight. A good label is also needed. I suggest the effigy of the Duc of Epernon since, it would appear, he used to come hunting on Padouën's land, but this matters little provided the Canots make good wine. The significant proportion of muscadelle in the wine should be noted.

Pajot (Domaine du)

Commune: Bommes. **Proprietor:** Alain Arnaud. **Size of vineyard:** 4 hectares. **Average age of vines:** 30 years. **Varieties:** 5% sauvignon, 90% sémillon, 5% muscadelle. **Production:** 6,000 bottles CB. **Direct sales and by mail order:** in France. Alain Arnaud, Le Marquis, Bommes, 33210 Langon. Tel. 56 63 66 90. *A fragmented estate which has a plot of 0.5 hectare in Yquem. Well-made wines which can be drunk young.*

Partarrieu (Château)

Commune: Fargues. **Proprietor:** Jacqueline Tuyttens-Laville. Consultant oenologist: Albert Bouyx. **Size of vineyard:** 18 hectares. **Average age of vines:** 30 to 40 years. **Varieties:** 100% sémillon. **Production:** 50 *tonneaux*, 30,000 bottles CB. **Direct sales and by mail order:** in France. Château Partarrieu, Fargues, 33210 Langon. **Retail sales.** *A discret silence veils the sizeable production of this property.*

Pascaud-Villefranche (Château)

Commune: Barsac. **Proprietor:** Société civile du Château Pascaud-Villefranche. Director: Pierre Pascaud. Manager: Fabien Pascaud. Consultant oenologist: Cadillac laboratory. **Size of vineyard:** 7.89 hectares. **Average age of vines:** 100 years. **Varieties:** 20% sauvignon, 75% sémillon, 5% muscadelle. **Production:** 25,500 bottles CB. **Visits:** tel. 56 27 16 09. **Direct sales and by mail order:** in France and abroad. M. Pascaud, Château Pascaud-Villefranche, Barsac, 33720 Podensac. **Retail sales:** through Bordeaux and a shipper in the United States.

In announcing that the average age of his vines is one hundred years, Pierre Pascaud is paying tribute to the achievement of the founder of the property, his grandfather Fabien Pascaud, who died thirty years ago. The two brothers who inherited it, Robert and Jean, preferred to divide the estate in two rather than run it jointly. Jean, Pierre's father, then created the name of Château Pascaud-Villefranche, now the responsibility of Fabien, one of his three sons. He himself is the estate manager of Château Suduiraut. The other two sons, Alain and Claude, are respectively manager of a *coopérative* in Béziers and cellar master at Château Coutet. The wine of Pascaud-Villefranche is a modern but well-made Barsac. It strives more for delicacy than maximum sweetness. Its concession to tradition is always to use "heavy" bottles and wooden boxes. The drinker will find a pleasing consistency in style and lively acidity, just right for stimulating the taste-buds. Moreover its sweetness does not exclude liveliness. On the contrary these two characteristics are combined in the perfect balance of a good Sauternes.

The third generation at work.

Pavillon (Clos du)

Commune: Preignac. **Proprietor:** Juliette Lacomme. Estate manager: M. Lacomme. Consultant oenologist: Pierre Sudraud. **Size of vineyard:** 0.44 hectares. **Average age of vines:** 20 years. **Varieties:** 33% sauvignon, 33% sémillon, 33% muscadelle. **Production:** 3 *barriques*, 1,000 bottles CB. **Direct sales and by mail order:** Clos du Pavillon, Preignac, 33210 Langon. Tel. 56 63 12 55. *The production of this little known cru, which is not mentioned in the 1986 Féret, is as limited as its distribution.*

Pebayle (Château)

Commune: Barsac. **Proprietor:** G.F.A. du Hayot. Consultant oenologist: Albert Bouyx. **Size of vineyard:** 7 hectares. **Average age of vines:** 25 to 30 years. **Varieties:** 25% sauvignon, 65% sémillon, 10% muscadelle. **Production:** 19 *tonneaux*, 25,000 bottles CB. **Direct sales and by mail order:** G.F.A. du Hayot, Château Andoyse, Barsac, 33720 Podensac. Tel. 56 27 15 37. **Retail sales.** *See Guiteronde du Hayot.*

Peillon-Claverie (Château)

Commune: Fargues. **Proprietors:** Odile Tachon and Pierre Dubourg. Consultant oenologist: C.E.I.OE. in Cadillac. **Size of vineyard:** 16 hectares. **Average age of vines:** 30 years. **Varieties:** 5% sauvignon, 90% sémillon, 5% muscadelle. **Production:** 30 barrels, 5,000 bottles CB. **Visits:** tel. 56 23 65 51. **Direct sales and by mail order:** in France. Château Peillon-Claverie, Fargues, 33210 Langon; or Pierre Dubourg, Ladaux, 33760 Targon. **Retail sales:** through Bordeaux. *In the Tachon and Dubourg families for four generations. A pleasant "little" Sauternes at a reasonable price.*

Pernaud (Château)

Commune: Barsac. **Proprietor:** G.F.A. Château Pernaud (M. and Madame B. Regelsperger). Estate manager and cellar master: Jean-Gabriel Jacolin. Vineyard manager: Jean-Bernard Jauberty. Manager: Isabelle Jacolin. Consultant oenologist: M. Llorca. **Size of vineyard:** 14.35 hectares. **Average age of vines:** 25 years. **Varieties:** 25% sauvignon, 70% sémillon, 5% muscadelle. **Production:** 45,000 bottles CB. **Visits:** M. Jacolin, tel. 56 27 26 52. **Direct sales:** Château Pernaud, Barsac, 33720 Podensac. **Retail sales:** brokers, commercial agents, private clients, Comtesse du Barry S.A. under the name Pey-Arnaud.

Local history relates that the Lur Saluces took refuge at Pernaud, one of their lesser properties, during the Revolution. This is quite improbable as far as the male side of the family goes, for during the Reign of Terror Claude-Henry, the Marquis of Lur Saluces, was guillotined in Bordeaux, while other members of the family had already emigrated. But it is possible that Françoise-Joséphine, the young widow of Comte Louis-Amédée de Lur Saluces (she was twenty in 1788, when he died as a result of a fall from his horse, and already the mother of a baby aged two) might have remained in the area in an attempt to preserve the family's assets. As Richard Olney says in his book on Yquem: "The stages of the rough road that the young Comtesse

152

during these years are thrown into uncertain focus by a paucity of documents". We know that she succeeded but we know nothing of how she lived between 1793 and the advent of the Empire.

Whatever the case, the Regelsperger family has owned this *cru* for three generations. The "château" is a charming little country house reigning alone in the middle of its vineyard, which covers fifteen hectares in one unbroken stretch. The Ciron flows at the foot of the vineyards, whose rows are as straight as a die. Philippe Couderc, the well-known wine and food columnist whose distinctive style so beguiles his readers, got it right when he recognized Pernaud as a very good Barsac. But he could not prevent himself from making an appalling pun on the names Pernaud and Pernod. Not to be outdone, I will now declare that Pernaud is a delicious *apéro [aperitif]*.

Perroy (Château) ♟ → Sigalas-Rabaud

Petit-Mayne (Château) ♟ → Caillou

Pey-Arnaud (Château) ♟ → Pernaud

Peyraguey (Cru)   ♛ ♛ ♛ ♛ ♛

Commune: Preignac. **Proprietors:** M. and Madame Marcel Duchamp, Preignac, 33210 Langon. Tel. 56 63 16 76. **Size of vineyard:** 2.5 hectares. **Average age of vines:** 30 years. **Varieties:** 16% sauvignon, 68% sémillon, 16% muscadelle. **Production:** 5 *tonneaux,* **Retail sales:** in bulk.

For the French painter Marcel Duchamp, one of the fathers of Surrealism and a companion of Picabia and Apollinaire, "a single exemplary gesture was worth a thousand times more than a thousand repetitions of the example." Apart from his majestic work *La Mariée mise à nu par ses célibataires, même* (The bride stripped bare by her bachelors even), he was also the inventor of the *"ready-made"*, one of the most famous being a bottle drip-rack in galvanized metal in the form of a tiara, "a disarming synthesis of invention and banality", as it was described by the art critic Marcel Jean. All this has nothing at all to do with the present-day production of Marcel Duchamp, the Preignac grower, apart from his having the same name and the bottle dryer. His Cru Peyraguey is marketed only in bulk. So it is a good illustration of the principle of banality according to Duchamp the surrealist. Perhaps Duchamp the grower should become a neo-realist and deliver his good, well-made wine in bottle.

Peyron (Château)

Commune: Fargues. **Proprietor:** Société du Château Peyron (Monsieur Chaumès), Saint-Pierre d'Aurillac, 33490 Saint-Macaire. **Size of vineyard:** 6.66 hectares. **Average age of vines:** 35 years. **Varieties:** 10% sauvignon, 88% sémillon, 2% muscadelle. **Production:** 17 *tonneaux*. **Retail sales:** in bulk. *This estate has chose a policy of maximum yields for commercial wines.*

sold in bulk

Piada (Château)

Commune: Barsac. **Proprietor:** Jean Lalande. **Size of vineyard:** 10 hectares. **Average age of vines:** 35 years. **Varieties:** 10% sauvignon, 90% sémillon. **Production:** 25 *tonneaux*, 19,000 bottles CB. **Visits:** daily, Sundays by appointment. Tel. 56 27 16 13. **Direct sales and by mail order:** in France. Château Piada, Barsac, 33720 Podensac. **Retail sales.**

"In 1941, Prunier's restaurant supplied Colonel Rémy with six bottles of Sauternes for members of the crew of a German submarine based in Lorient. Thanks to the effects produced by these precious wines, the secret agent Alphonse Tanguy was able to spirit away the German defence plans. Thirty years later, Marcel Achard, recalling this exploit at Prunier's, awarded a symbolic 'Order of the Nation' to Châteaux Filhot, Suduiraut, La Tour Blanche, Piada, and Haut-Bergeron. On the same occasion, he dubbed Yquem a 'Compagnon de la Libération'. "(I have already quoted from this, one of my favourite passages, in Haut-Bergeron). A wine that becomes a hero as the result of a war is hardly an everyday event. But the wine of Piada seems to be destined for the pages of history, since it was also one of the favourite *crus* of the "father of the people", Joseph Vissarionovich Djugashvili, otherwise known as Stalin. This just goes to show that even the toughest dictators have their weaknesses.

Piada, the property of the Lur Saluces before the Revolution, and afterwards sold and attached to Château Coutet, regained its independence at the end of the nineteenth century. Amédée Jean Lalande, the father of today's proprietor Jean Lalande, bought it in 1940. I do not know where my friend Hugh Johnson found 30% of riesling growing in the vineyard (*Hugh Johnson's Wine Companion,* Mitchell Beazley, 1983). Perhaps he over-indulged in the *cru* before identifying and counting the vines...or perhaps it was a mistake in the French edition published in 1984. One must always give one's friends the benefit of the doubt.

The style of Piada respects that of each different vintage. Sometimes it is fine and elegant, sometimes vigorous and opulent. That is enough to demonstrate Jean Lalande's love of nature: "The richness in alcohol and reducing sugars varies from year to year depending on the climate and the quality of the botrytis." He endeavours to reap the best possible benefit from these changing factors and to make use of them without distorting them. The proof is to be found in recent vintages which are certainly all identifiably Piada, though each has its own personality. Jean Lalande can describe better his '82 better than I can: when he says it is "very complete", he means that maximum quality is present at every level. Talking about the '83, which is marvellous, he says modestly that it is "rich and complex – but lacking in

5. Château Piada — Barsac
Les Vendanges. — La dernière Comporte (1904)

Marès Bx.

A festive end to harvesting in 1904.

vigour". In '84, he bottled six hectolitres of Château Piada: "A great success considering the year!" Jean Lalande is as genuine as his wine – and he is also something of a poet:

> Pride of the gems of Sauternes and Barsac,
> It gleams iridescent with brilliance so pure,
> And charms eye and palate, a sumptuous liqueur,
> Divine, warm and golden, as rich as velour:
> Adorable nectar, true gold of Barsac.

And he concludes "Château Piada always appeals to the imagination."

Pilotte (Clos)

Commune: Fargues. **Proprietor:** Guy Dupeyron. Fargues, 33210 Langon. Tel. 56 63 07 27. Consultant oenologist: Jean-Paul Pauquet. **Size of vineyard:** 7 hectares. **Average age of vines:** from 5 to 30 years. **Varieties:** 10% sauvignon, 80% sémillon, 10% muscadelle. **Production:** 19 *tonneaux*. **Retail sales:** in bulk. *A few sales here and there by "word of mouth", but Madame Dupeyron's children decided not to continue the work after her. In 1990, the estate was leased to Château Rieussec.*

Piot David (Château)

Commune: Barsac. **Proprietor:** Jean-Luc David. **Size of vineyard:** 7 hectares. **Average age of vines:** 35 years. **Varieties:** 15% sauvignon, 85% sémillon. **Production:** *18 tonneaux,* 22,000 bottles CB. **Visits:** by appointment, tel. 56 62 97 30. **Sales by mail, order:** in France. Monsieur David, Château Poncet, 33410 Omet. **Retail sales:** through Bordeaux and for export.

The one distinctive feature the Sauternes region presents to the visitor is the stone walls which border its highways and byways giving the surrounding countryside a restricted, even enclosed appearance. In a vine-growing region where harvesting is carried out at the latest possible moment, it is an elementary precaution to try to prevent marauders from pilfering the golden grapes. Thus the Piot David vineyard, lies in one unbroken stretch, entirely walled around. The only way in is through the main gateway or else to take a ladder with you... unless of course you land by parachute. The David family arrived here in 1961. Jean-Luc David has been sole owner since 1983. Several such young growers have taken up the reins over the last ten or so years to restore the fortunes of Barsac and Sauternes. Generally, the wine of David is heady, very full with floral and fruity aromas, with a tendency to develop further as it ages. It represents excellent value in Barsac, and indeed throughout the world. As Jean-Luc matures both in age and experience, the wine let produces gets better and better. The time is drawing near when Château Piot David will justifiably deserve its four glasses.

Pleytegeat (Château) ⚓ → Romer du Hayot

Pouteau (Cru)

sold in bulk

Commune: Fargues. **Proprietor:** Raymond Tastet, Pouteau, Fargues, 33210 Langon. Tel. 56 63 11 91. **Size of vineyard:** 1.02 hectares. **Varieties:** 20% sauvignon, 70% sémillon, 10% muscadelle. **Production:** 2.5 *tonneaux.* **Retail sales:** in bulk.

Pouteau (Domaine de)

Commune: Fargues. **Proprietors:** Monsieur and Madame Hubert Ferchi. Consultant oenologist: Jean-Paul Pauquet. **Size of vineyard:** 3 hectares. **Average age of vines:** 50 years. **Varieties:** 10% sauvignon, 80% sémillon, 10% muscadelle. **Production:** *tonneaux,* 8,000 bottles CB. **Visits:** preferably by appointment, tel. 56 63 41 85. **Direct sales and by mail order:** in France. Domaine de Pouteau, Preignac, 33210 Langon.

This château bears the same name as Jean-Luc Pouteau, winner of the title of "the world's best *sommelier* "in 1983. This is no dishonour to anyone, neither to Gaston Lenôtre's *sommelier*, who has his name printed in gold leaf on a label of sterling quality, nor to the Ferchi household, who care for the scattered and sunny plots of vines like so many Japanese gardens. They proudly inform visitors that the estate has been in Monsieur Ferchi's family "forever". Since the 1975 vintage they have bottled their production themselves. Aged in wood and lovingly tended, the wine has a delicious fruitiness. Both to the nose and the palate, it opens out to reveal a lovely strong essence of typically botrytized aromas.

Prost (Château)

Commune: Barsac. **Proprietor:** Jean Perromat, Château Prost, Barsac, 33720 Podensac. Tel. 56 27 01 13. Vineyard manager: Dominique Labourgade. Cellar master: Jean-Luc Bernède. Consultant oenologist: M. Llorca. **Size of vineyard:** 11 hectares. **Average age of vines:** 24 years. **Varieties:** 20% sauvignon, 65% sémillon, 15% muscadelle. **Production:** 32 *tonneaux*, 30,000 bottles CB. **Retail sales throught the trade.**

In the heart of the village of Barsac, not far from the church, is a little sixteenth-century baronial mansion, with corner towers and external spiral staircase. In the eighteenth century the geographer Belleyme, called this spot Madélis. In fact that was the ancient name of the site, which is redolent of history, as witness the many Gallo-Roman remains. The present name of Prost perpetuates the memory of the German négociant of that name who did business in the rue des Argentiers in Bordeaux in 1612. It might be said that for a wine merchant to be called "Prost" is as fitting as "Salmon" for a fishmonger! Jean Perromat, who used to be the mayor of Cérons for several years, has run the estate since 1966. The soil is composed of a very shallow layer of clayey siliceous gravel laid down in the Quaternary era on a bed of Jurassic asteroidian limestone. The presence of this limestone manifests itself in a particular liveliness in the wine of Prost and a flinty flavour much sought after by many drinkers, among them myself and which is not often encountered in the *terroir* of Sauternes. The Perromats are careful and dedicated growers who can be relied on. Their wines, not only in Barsac but in Cérons and the Graves too, are worthy of the highest regard.

Pugneau (Cru)

Commune: Fargues. **Proprietor:** Guy Labarbe. Consultant oenologist: Pierre Sudraud. **Size of vineyard:** 3.3 hectares. **Varieties:** 20% sauvignon, 60% sémillon, 20% muscadelle. **Production:** 9 *tonneaux*, 3,500 bottles CB. **Visits:** by appointment only. Tel. 56 63 09 06. **Direct sales and by mail order:** in France. Guy Labarbe, Les Tuileries, Fargues, 33210 Langon. *Despite substantial yields, the wines bottled by Guy Labarbe - who has patiently bought this little estate plot after plot since 1950 - are more than pleasant.*

Rabaud-Promis (Château)

1er cru classé

Commune: Bommes. **Proprietor:** G.F.A. du Château Rabaud-Promis. Estate manager: Philippe Dejean. Consultant oenologist: Pierre Sudraud. **Size of vineyard:** 32 hectares. **Average age of vines:** 35 to 40 years. **Varieties:** 18% sauvignon, 80% sémillon, 2% muscadelle. **Production:** 48,000 bottles CB. **Visits:** Monday to Friday from 9 a.m. to 6 p.m. Tel. 56 63 60 52. **Direct sales and by mail order:** in France. Château Rabaud-Promis, Bommes, 33210 Langon. **Retail sales:** through Bordeaux.

The first time in my life I was "one over the eight" was thanks to Rabaud-Promis, which my family then owned. My father, Pierre Ginestet, had taken my brother and me with him on his tour of inspection of the vineyards. In the morning we called at Clos Fourtet where we had lunch. The estate manager's wife, Madame Banquel, had prepared us a *court-bouillon* of lamprey (her own recipe). We were allowed just a drop of wine in the cellar. At that time, the wine spent at least two years in the *barrique*. If my memory serves me correctly, this memorable day was in the summer of 1947. So the Clos Fourtet we drank must have been the '45. I was eleven. It was intensely hot. Then we set off for Sauternes, crossing the Entre-deux-Mers region and the Garonne between Cadillac and Cérons. It was quite an excursion. I slept a little in the old black Citroen.

When we arrived at Rabaud, we went round the vineyard. Then we went into the cellars. Their natural coolness contrasted sharply with the blazing heat outside. We felt more at ease. My father told us to be good while he went away to go over some papers with the estate manager. My brother and I went once or twice round

Rabaud has excellent terrain, perfect for producing wine of the highest quality.

the cellar inspecting the casks. We stopped in front of a shelf on which hung a glass pipette and a few wine glasses for tasting. We knew how these were used thanks to Marcel Grangerou, the cellar master at Château Margaux. In the cellars where the *barriques* of Rabaud's new wine lay, the glass bungs were uppermost. This meant that to remove a bung to introduce a pipette into a cask was mere child's play. We competed with each other to see who could draw off the wine without spilling a drop and then fill the glasses holding the pipette as high up as possible. Then we drank and repeated the game. When father reappeared, we were blind drunk. The journey home was spent on the floor of the Citroën. My mother put us both to bed without further ado. She was not amused but my brother and I were in radiantly good humour.

In 1950 Pierre Ginestet sold the property to Raymond-Louis Lanneluc. Since then a financial company has been set up, run by his grandson, Philippe Dejean. I remember Rabaud's 1950 vintage. It was exceptional. At a triangular blind tasting at Château Margaux, it beat Yquem and Schloss Johannisberg of the same year, and this in the presence of the Marquis Bertrand de Lur Saluces and Prince Metternich.

Since then, Rabaud's vintages have had their ups and downs as regards both quality and quantity. The *cru* was courageously declassified as Sauternes in the years '72, '73, '74 and '75. The high percentage of clay in the soil gives the wine an exceptional power when the climate is favourable. But it is very susceptible to years of cold and rain.

Contrary to the opinion of several distinguished critics, I find that Rabaud-Promis's production over the course of the last ten years merits high praise.

Raymond-Lafon (Château)   ♟ ♟ ♟ ♟ ♟

Commune: Sauternes. **Proprietors:**Société du Château Raymond-Lafon – Famille Meslier. Manager: Marie-Françoise Meslier. Wine-maker: Charles-Henri Meslier. Director of public relations and sales: Jean-Pierre Meslier. **Size of vineyard:** 15 hectares. **Average age of vines:** 40 years. **Varieties:** 20% sauvignon, 80% sémillon. **Production:** 18,000 bottles CB.**Visits:** by appointment only. Tel. 56 63 21 02. Fax: 56 63 19 58. **Direct sales and by mail order:** in France. Château Raymond-Lafon, Sauternes, 33210 Langon.

Towards the end of the last century the local notables of Langon used to meet regularly. The lawyer and the chemist, the coalman and the hat-maker, the man who imported colonial foodstuffs and the press agent for *La Petite Gironde* would be there. The *sous-préfet* himself ever deigned to put in an appearance at the weekly assembly to empty a glass of absinthe and to give the honourable gentlemen the   159

There is something rather English about the green silhouette of Raymond-Lafon.

benefit of his enlightened opinion on the progress of the railways or the probable development in wine prices. But then, soon after the law was passed on March 16, 1915 prohibiting the manufacture and sale of absinthe, the circle was disbanded. It had some distinguished wines in its cellars. A group of wily businessmen bought them up and founded a firm by the name of *Etablissements de l'Union*. Among the documentation which Jean-Pierre Meslier likes to display today is the sale price of the 1922 vintage, Yquem 1918, quoted at 15 francs per bottle, followed by Châteaux Suduiraut 1916 at 15 francs, Raymond-Lafon 1917 at 14 francs, Lafaurie-Peyraguey 1918 at 13 francs, and so on. As for the wines of the Médoc, they hardly made any impact – Château Margaux 1913 was priced at 12 francs, Montrose 1912 at 9.50 francs and the excellent Branaire 1916 could command only 9 francs! At this time, the proprietor of Château Raymond-Lafon was Louis Pontallier. He was a master grower and his Sauternes *cru*, which was not classified, outclassed many of the *Premiers*.

Following this, Raymond-Lafon went through a troubled period. Indeed, its former glory was in total eclipse at the time when Francine and Pierre Meslier bought the property from Dr Bourdier of Preignac. That was in October 1972. Since that time, Raymond-Lafon has made astonishing progress. It must be said that Pierre Meslier, former estate manager of Château d'Yquem, adopts the same methods and care he practised on the King of Sauternes for his own *cru*. With an average annual yield of 9 hectolitres, his 15 hectares of light gravel distil approximately 18,000 bottles per vintage, a production which could be described as homoeopathic, representing just one glass of wine from each vine.

The vineyard lies between distinguished neighbours: Yquem to the south and the east; Suduiraut to the north; and Rabaud-Promis, Sigalas Rabaud, Lafaurie-Peyraguey and Rayne Vigneau to the west, not far from the Ciron with its botrytizing morning mists. The proportion of varieties favours the sémillon. The wine is kept in oak *barriques* only, of which a third are renewed every year. It remains in the wood for at least three years, four at the most.

The only wines permitted to bear the name of "Raymond-Lafon" are those which are of finest quality. The others are ruthlessly declassified as "Sauternes" pure and simple. In 1974, Château Raymond-Lafon was conspicuous by its absence: the proprietor himself refused to accord the name to the wine. All this in the quest for perfection. The '75, which is practically unobtainable today, is a dazzling example: iridescent gold, a complex nose of broom blossom, vanilla and linden, honey with a hundred perfumes, a massive, almost enormous attack in the mouth, unctuous and powerful, heady, with an unending finish. Like myself, the great *sommelier* Jean-Luc Pouteau was staggered at the wines of the Meslier family. He rhapsodized particularly about the '78: "Limpid gold, bright, very rich, an intense aromatic nose, in the mouth aromas of crystallized lemon, quince jelly, harmonious and mellow." This is echoed by the opinions of Hugh Johnson and Robert Parker. The first considers Raymond-Lafon "first class". The second goes further, stressing that one bottle costs less than half a bottle of Yquem. We should recognize and pay tribute to the art of the Mesliers, not only Pierre and Francine but their children too, Marie-Françoise, Charles-Henri and Jean-Pierre. This family is motivated by a desire for perfection. The nectar they put in bottles is truly worth its weight in the gold.

Raymond Louis (Domaine) ☖ → Cameron

Rayne Vigneau (Château de)

1er cru classé

Commune: Bommes. **Proprietor:** S.C. du Château de Rayne Vigneau. Director: Jean-Pierre Angliviel de La Beaumelle. Manager: Patrice Bandiera. Estate manager: Patrick Eymery. Consultant oenologist: Bernard Monteau. **Size of vineyard:** 65 hectares. **Average age of vines:** 22 years. **Varieties:** 25% sauvignon, 75% sémillon. **Production:** 120,000 bottles CB. **Visits:** weekdays from 9 a.m. to 4 p.m. Mestrezat S.A., tel. 56 52 11 46. **Retail sales:** through Bordeaux.

In 1855 this *cru* was called simply Vigneau, and it was under this name that it was classified as a *premier cru*. In 1860, Gabriel de Pontac inherited it from his aunt, the *Baronne* de Rayne, and he handed it down in 1892 to his nephew Albert, who created the name Rayne Vigneau. After him, the estate was run by his son-in-law, *Vicomte* de Roton. A journalist and writer passionately interested in nature and the region he devoted a large part of his life to categorizing the soil of his vineyards and gathering a prodigious collection of minerals, from fossilized oysters to agate and different varieties of quartz. My old friend Raymond Dumay recalls his visit to the "pebble gentleman":

"After travelling slowly through the vineyards, I arrived in the Sauternes region and knocked at the door of one of the world's *.premiers crus*: Château Rayne Vigneau. I was impelled by something more than the love of wine – my childhood passion for agates. I had at one time gathered a superb collection: to be precise, all those to be found in my own village. But I was only a child: Château Rayne Vigneau has ten thousand.

"A servant, who reminded me of Marcel Proust's Françoise, opened the door to me: 'Ah! The gentleman has come for the pebbles' she said in a certain tone of voice.

"Viscount de Roton speaks of his stones more affectionately. An old schoolfellow of the writer Claudel, Laureate of the Institute and illustrator of the *Chansons de Bilitis* and the *Iliad* in the style of Greek vases, my host drops everything to talk to me of his land.

161

Entirely independent of the estate, the château is the residence of Vicomte de Roton.

While I admire the amazing designs of nature with my eye glued to microscope or magnifying glass, he, like some Homeric hero, recites the list of his discoveries: agates striped and beribboned, crystalline agates regularly striped agates, eye agates, moss agates, Venus hair agates, landscape agates, fortification agates, white sapphires, the golden yellow topazes known as Alençon diamonds, rock crystal, streaked and banded oölites, smoky quartz, lydites, calcites, aragonites. . . No, I could never list the fifteen thousand pieces in this museum of natural jewellery. That pleasure should be left for its creator, the man who, after having thousands of samples cut, distributed them to all the geological museums in France and throughout the world. They stand up to comparison with the most famous minerals from Brazil, Madagascar and Australia. Thus capricious Nature showers us with things of great beauty. But few of us have, like the Vicomte de Roton, the idea of holding out our hands to catch them in the form of pebbles.

"My visit ended with the presentation of the final jewel in the museum, the only one which needed no cutting: a glass of Sauternes, luscious, mellow, almost syrupy, amber yet transparent, a marvellous wine which, it is claimed, has no equal.

"At dusk, I left Bommes-en-Sauternes, thinking gratefully of Armand Got who had sent me to the 'prince of nectar and gems'." (Raymond Dumay, *Ma route d'Aquitaine,* Paris 1949)

At Universal Exhibition in 1867, Rayne Vigneau had the honour of being named champion of Sauternes in a duel with the best wine from the Rhineland. The twenty expert tasters were unanimous and Rayne Vigneau triumphed. The report of the competition records: "It would be ungracious to mention that the wine from the Rhine came from one single *barrique*, harvested grape by grape and carefully selected from the whole crop." The winner was a 1861. It features in the series of Rayne Vigneaus for which the famous gastronome André Simon drew up a list of alcoholic strengths. His statistics cover 73 vintages starting with the 1840, and reveal an average alcohol content of 14° (the most outstanding year was 1875, with 17°, and the least satisfactory was 1910, with 12). The density of the liqueur varied between 3° and 5° depending on the vintage.

In 1961 the vineyard was separated from the château. Ten years later, after passing through the hands of Paul Raoux, it has come under the care of the firm of Mestrezat, through another firm administered by Jean-Pierre Angliviel de La Beaumelle. Without any doubt, Rayne Vigneau has made a spectacular recovery over the last ten years. With a policy of smaller yields, it could continue its progress. The '88 vintage undoubtedly marks a decisive stage in this progress. Naturally this was a great year throughout the Sauternes appellation. However, the '88 of Rayne Vigneau is outstandingly successful.

Rieussec (Château)

1er cru classé

Commune: Fargues. Proprietor: S.A. Château Rieussec. Consultant oenologists: Messrs. Bouyx and Peynaud. Size of vineyard: 66 hectares. Average age of vines: 30 years. Varieties: 18% sauvignon, 80% sémillon, 2% muscadelle. Production: about 80,000 bottles CB. Visits: Monday to Friday by appointment. Tel. 56 63 31 02. Château Rieussec, Fargues, 33210 Langon. Retail sales: in the traditional way.

Rieussec occupies an elevated position to the west of the commune of Fargues of which it is the only *Premier cru classé*. In 1985 Albert Vuillier found a prestigious partner when he became the associate of the Rothschild family. As Vuillier has the experience and Rothschild the money, no one can doubt that the wines born of this union will be remarkable. When the Domaines Rothschild give their name to a label, they are anxious for it to be highly regarded. So we shall soon see the drinkable results of this association which I can only applaud.

To return to the past, without imposing on the reader the apparently endless list of previous owners (although I have it available for those who wish to consult it), I would like to quote from a little-known text. It is taken from a book by Charles Mayet, rarely found today, entitled *Le Vin de France* and published at the end of the last century by Jouvet and Co. (Librairie Furne). Mayet was a prolific writer for the newspaper *Le Temps* newspaper, with a style that was often dazzling and sometimes biting. He took up the cudgels for viticulture in the south and he was one of the forerunners of the philosophy of the co-operative system. In this extract he relates a "historic meeting":

"It was a memorable evening.

"With that boldness characteristic of youth, Australia entered the lists against France. Wines against wines. A room in Voisin's restaurant had been chosen for

The arrival of the Rothschilds gives this exceptional soil a new lease of life.

the field of battle. Proud of the success they had had against certain foreign wines at the 1889 Exhibition, the Australians had aimed higher. Having got the better of their competitors from other countries, they courageously sat down at the table in the heart of Paris, with glass in hand, challenging our great *crus* and entrusting to a privileged few the delicate mission of being impartial judges of the contest. I was seated between Prince Galitzine, the president of the wine section at the Exhibition, and an Australian, a big cattle breeder for his sins. The meal was lengthy and exquisite. As soon as the first course was served, the *sommelier* was asked to serve the Australian wine. It was a white, with an agreeable colour rather like that of straw. It was lacking in limpidity and its appearance and its vague perfume were suggestive of those wines from the borders of the Rhine of which Aurélien Scholl recently said that they seemed to have ripened by moonlight. When the waiter had filled the glasses, all the guests drank together. Australia's twenty or so representatives remained silent, studying our reactions. 'It is excellent', said Prince Galitzine.

"And indeed, excellent it was. Imagine a full-bodied wine, rather new, with many good points and many defects, the product of virgin soil with excesses of good and bad elements. Voisin replied with a wine of Sauternes, a Château Rieussec of a good vintage; which one exactly, I do not recall. 'A fine colour', said an Australian, turning his glass round between his fingers in front of the candle flames.

"And a fine colour it was indeed. It was one of those admirable wines of which you could say it was sunshine in the bottle. The light from the candelabra was transformed behind it as if under the lens of an optical instrument, turning it into 164 a star of extraordinary brilliance. It had the limpidity of a precious jewel, a warm colour of rich and rare distinction, pure gold embroidered with fine pearls. The Australian who was presiding at the meal raised his glass: 'Gentlemen', he said, 'it is perhaps presumptuous of us to ask you to compare our wines with yours. But we have worked conscientiously and we feel we can be justly proud. Whatever fate awaits us now, we are sure you will do justice to our efforts.'

"Having said this, he put the glass to his lips. All the diners followed suit. There was a whole minute of complete silence. Each man looked at his neighbour with an air of astonished rapture. The wine, delicate and mellow, had an indefinable delicacy and savour. Centuries of civilization and culture were revealed in the perfect harmony of its make-up, whereas the Australian wine had an almost barbaric fire. You might have said it was like one of Horace's odes compared with the song of a primitive bard. The big cattle breeder on my right smiled, whispering in my ear: 'We are beaten.'

"No one dwelled on such an easily won victory. One fact however told something of its character: all the glasses into which the waiter had served Australian wine remained as they were after the first tasting, that is three parts full. No one took another sip. The French wines were masters of the field of battle.

"If I recall this combat in which the number of dead was considerable on our side, it is particularly in order to highlight the truly extraordinary quality of the great white wines of Bordeaux. The Sauternes region owes its worldwide reputation to them."

Though perhaps a little lengthy,this extract serves to illustrate as nothing else could that competitions between French and foreign wines are not the creation of a contemporary journalistic fashion. In other words, Gault and Millau have invented nothing and their "Olympiades des vins" merely ensure the continuation of these chivalrous tournaments between good *crus* and proprietors brought up in the school of "fair play".

CHATEAU RIEUSSEC

1ᵉʳ GRAND CRU

SAUTERNES

From all this I draw one conclusion: indisputably, during preceding centuries, and especially in the eighteenth and nineteenth, French wines came out on top in these international competitions. It is important that this "privilege" should continue, particularly in Barsac and Sauternes which, in the past, have proved their dazzling supremacy over and over again. Laws and administrative rulings will not resolve the question. The continuing supremacy of Barsac and Sauternes wines is something to be striven for.

The arrival of the Rothschilds gives this exceptional property by the Ciron a new lease of life. Over and above their financial interests, for which they are of course more than competent, I hope that they are fully aware of their responsibility to produce an exemplary wine. I have confidence in the future. "Rieussec, moreover, produces wines which greatly resemble those of Yquem" (Charles Cocks, 1868).

Rolland (Château de)

Commune: Barsac. **Proprietor:** G.F.A. Château de Rolland. Directors: Jean and Pierre Guignard. **Size of vineyard:** 18 hectares. **Average age of vines:** 30 years. **Varieties:** 20% sauvignon, 60% sémillon, 20% muscadelle. **Production:** *40 tonneaux* 48,000 bottles CB. **Visits:** by appointment, Jean Guignard, tel. 56 27 15 02. **Direct sales and by mail order:** in France. Jean and Pierre Guignard S.C.A., Château de Rolland, Barsac, 33720 Podensac. **Retail sales:** through Bordeaux.

If we can observe, sometimes with regret, the lack of commercial initiative on the part of Sauternes producers, we may equally well observe that the efforts made by a few of them are in sharp contrast. Undoubtedly, Jean and Pierre Guignard belong to this small band and their endeavours to get themselves better known are as unaffected as they are dynamic, even if certain churlish people find them excessive. But in a region of ancestral châteaux where leaks are more common than restored gargoyles, they have had the simple yet ingenious idea of constructing a little tasting room in rustic style beside of the R.N. 113, which links Bordeaux with Toulouse. Here the tourist can take a break and find a genuinely cordial welcome. He can taste the *cru* in congenial surroundings and continue his journey again, armed with a few carefully packaged bottles. The Château de Rolland itself is a smart hostelry in which a young but go-ahead executive of a small but profitable business would not feel out of place.

As for the viticultural side of the estate, this is extremely well looked after and yields a wine which holds its place more than honourably in the ranks of the *bourgeois supérieurs*. By its very size it is no longer a small concern; by its quality it is better than a simple Barsac. Since 1971 Jean and Pierre Guignard have striven to give their label the image of a revitalized classicism. Recent vintages demonstrate that this was a worthy and justified aim, even in off years.

By its very size, the estate of Château de Rolland is no longer a minor concern.

Romer du Hayot (Château)

2e cru classé

Commune: Fargues. **Proprietor:** GFA du Hayot. Director: André du Hayot. Consultant oenologist: A. Bouyx. **Size of vineyard:** 25 hectares. **Average age of vines:** 30 years. **Varieties:** 25% sauvignon, 65% sémillon, 10% muscadelle. **Production:** 80,000 bottles CB. **Visits:** Monday to Friday. Tel. 56 27 15 37. **Direct sales and by mail order:** in France. M. du Hayot, Château Guiteronde, Barsac. 33720 Podensac. **Retail sales:** in the traditional way.

The motorway "des Deux-Mers" was responsible for razing to the ground the old cellars and Château Romer itself, which has since transferred its working buildings to Château Guiteronde in Barsac (see above). This blow of fate was not the first. Romer, a very old name with a high reputation in the old business quarters of the Chartrons, has had to suffer the ravages of complex inheritances, and has been subdivided again and again. Up until 1977 there were two "Château Romers", one dependent on Roger Farges and the other on André du Hayot. The latter took the Farges estate on rental and production is now united as in the time of Count Auguste de la Myre-Mory, who made it a *deuxième cru classé* in 1855. Romer du Hayot's wine is typical of the Sauternes modern school. Fermentation and ageing in enamelled stainless steel vats; cold treatment with two filterings; and relatively early bottling. Its original character is perhaps hidden behind the standardization of the product. But it has its own style, which may or may not please. And then, we should not always systematically take the part of the Ancients against the Moderns, for while the Ancients make things move forward by pushing, the Moderns do so by pulling: it can be just as efficient a method of locomotion.

Roumieu (Château)

Commune: Barsac. **Proprietor:** Catherine Craveia-Goyaud. Consultant oenologist: Pierre Sudraud. **Size of vineyard:** 14 hectares. **Average age of vines:** 25 to 30 years. **Varieties:** 5% sauvignon, 95% sémillon. **Production:** 45,000 bottles CB. **Direct sales:** in France. Madame Craveia-Goyaud, Barsac, 33720 Podensac. Tel. 56 27 21 01. **Retail sales:** through Bordeaux and Libourne.

It is well documented that Roumieu was a mediaeval hamlet in the parish of Barsac. A variety of traces, superimposed one upon the other or juxtaposed side by side, bear witness to this; the most recent dating from the eighteenth century. According to the proprietor of the *cru*, the name Roumieu means "a point on the pilgrims' way to Santiago de Compostella". To support this assertion, she reminds us that the Moors called the pilgrims Roumis. This is how history is written and how etymology becomes an inexact science. The original use of the word Roumi was as the name given to the Turks by the Persians and Mongols (*Encyclopédie*, 1765). So it meant the people subject to Rome. Later it changed and was adopted by the Muslims to refer to Christians. It must be said that in the meantime the majority of the Romans had become Catholics. But until about the fifth century a "Romaeus" was simply 167

A practice now dying out: ageing the wine in oval barrels known as "foudres".

a pilgrim, also admittedly of course throughout the duration of the *pax Romana*, a pilgrim could not go on pilgrimage to any place other than Rome.

Roumieu very probably was one of the staging posts for the pilgrims on the way to Compostella. The Gascon tongue, whose roots are in mediaeval low Latin, leaves no doubt as to the meaning of the place. "Roumìu" definitly means "pilgrim". Roumieu is certainly where these pilgrims met up. The worship of the relics of St James began in about the year 900. It was in the eleventh and twelfth centuries that this form of religion took such a hold as to affect the whole of Europe. According to their "camì roumìu", or "pilgrims' way", the 'Jacobites' crossed the river from north to south at Blaye, Bourg, Langoiran, Loupiac or La Réole. Roumieu was on the left bank opposite Loupiac. This fragment of history in no way implies that the vineyard in Barsac was linked at the time with the pilgrims. But it does prove how old the site is as a human settlement. And it all goes to explain the *coquille Saint-Jacques* adorning the label of Roumieu.

Château Roumieu was for a long time considered the best non-classified *cru* in Barsac. Its reputation in the world of the Chartrons was very high at the beginning of this century. The Second World War and the years following brought difficulties in their wake, as was the case for many other properties in the region. In 1983 Madame Craveia-Goyaud took on the running of the estate, succeeding her father Pierre Goyaud. Her family has been present here since the beginning of the eighteenth century. She faces every challenge with energy and high notions of the ideal quality of a Barsac wine.

In my personal cellar, along with a collection of odd bottles, I knew I had a Roumieu 1934. Following an author's whim, I unearthed the bottle before dinner to stand it upright in the door of the fridge: my office would not be complete without this a fridge which, when I am lacking inspiration, assures me a supply of refreshment. It was something new and unusual for me to drink a wine at the moment of writing about it. But once does not constitute a habit. Moreover, I had only one bottle of Roumieu left. I think it came from my grandfather. That evening I was grateful to him for not having drunk it himself. It was fifty-three years old. Fernand Ginestet would have been one hundred and sixteen that evening. In the still of the night, the cork made an engaging "pop". It was clean, as unspotted brown and rock-solid as befits Portuguese cork of its age. The wine seemed to have oxidized. It had been cooling for about two hours. Had it been clearer when I took it out of the cellar? Difficult to say. Its temperature must have been between eight and ten degrees. That was all right. The label had been ruined by mould; doubtless the revenge of botrytis which, like a silent ghost with no chains to rattle, had licked the old gold lithograph and spoiled its appearance. If you knew what it was, you could read the word "Roumieu". The year was not visible to the eye but I had long since known it. And on the cork a confirming "4" could be read. I thought for a moment of the cellar worker who had seen to its being rolled under the branding die like a cigar-maker rolling a Partagas on her thigh. Was she young or old? Did her husband, in all probability a vigneron, like ham and pea soup? I would have liked to know all this and many other things besides, to be able to relate them to you. All I know is that I poured the Roumieu' 34 into a glass made by Baccarat some thirty years ago. I still smile at the thought of this charming ink-well of a bottle. I wanted to dip a brush into it to scrawl on my paper and create a (splendid) stain with the handwritten caption: "This is Roumieu!" But you, gentle reader, would not have taken me seriously, so I drank the wine to your health. That evening, I raised my glass to the health of those who love Barsac wines. Roumieu is a Barsac of the very best, even if it is not a *cru classé*.

I swirled the wine round. It seemed heavy. Almost viscous. Deep amber. Burnt topaz. It was awaiting my pleasure, which I finally knew that evening. There. I drew in that air of another time and I tasted. Something different. A way of being, possessing and loving; all dignified verbs which should never be lost from our language.

I should like to leave the last word on this *cru* to my very good friend Michael Broadbent, who in 1980 published his *Great Vintage Wine Book* (Mitchell Beazley), in which he sums up the innumerable tastings of his brilliant career at Christie's. This is how be described a Château Roumieu 1953, tasted in October 1979: " A little-seen Barsac, perfect capsule, label, branded cork and level: lovely colour, very bright, positive gold with hint of lemon; rich but delicate bouquet, honeyed Semillon, slight twist of lemon-peel acidity on nose and end taste; fairly sweet still, medium light, soft and very flavoury some fat but refreshing. Dry finish. Just caught before its decline."

Roûmieu-Lacoste (Château) ♈ ♈ ♈ ♈ ♈

Commune: Barsac. **Proprietor:** S.C.E. Bouchet Dubourdieu & Fils. Vineyard manager: Guy Desqueyroux. Consultant oenologist: Albert Bouyx. **Size of vineyard:** 12 hectares. **Average age of vines:** 30 years. **Varieties:** 3% sauvignon, 84% sémillon, 13% muscadelle. **Production:** 37,000 bottles CB. **Visits:** Hervé Dubourdieu, tel. 56 27 16 29. **Direct sales and by mail order:** in France and abroad. S.C.E. Bouchet Dubourdieu & Fils, Château Roûmieu-Lacoste, Barsac, 33720 Podensac. **Retail sales.**

In about 1900 the Roumieu estate was split into three parts. André Dubourdieu managed to acquire one of them. To distinguish it from the others, he added the name of "Lacoste", from the name of his grandfather who was a grower in the last century. Hervé Dubourdieu, the son of the house, has a wine list from Ledoyen's restaurant dating from 1914. On it, we read:

Château Margaux	1900	15 Frs
Château Roumieu	1900	15 Frs
Château Haut Brion	1900	15 Frs

"We benefit from the same qualities of soil as all the Barsac *Premiers Crus*" chorus the Dubourdieus. They are right. Here are tasting notes on a few recent years:

1976: An attractive golden colour without excessive coloration. Nose of plum. Fine freshness. A rather bitter but persistent finish.

1978: A light gold colour. A nose of new oak with a hint of hawthorn blossom. Botrytis can be detected and the roundness in the mouth is agreeable.

1983: Ah! A whole olfactory alphabet, from acacia and pineapple to vanilla and plant-life. Power, charm, elegance. A distinction which speaks for itself.

1986: Golden straw-yellow colour. Nose of vanilla and spices, aromas of honey and sweet almond. All the vitality of a Barsac with a broad balance between alcohol and liquorosity. Very elegant, refined vintage.

1988: A wine of great breeding in prospect, much admired in professional tastings.

1989: According to M. Dubourdieu, the last wine of such quality was in 1937.

Rouquette (Château)

Commune: Preignac. **Proprietor:** Hubert Dufour. Consultant oenologist: Pierre Sudraud. **Size of vineyard:** 6.4 hectares. **Average age of vines:** 45 years. **Varieties:** 5% sauvignon, 90% sémillon, 5% muscadelle. **Production:** 18 *tonneaux*, 55.000 bottles CB. **Direct sales and by mail order:** in France. Hubert Dufour, Château Rouquette, Preignac, 33210 Langon. Tel. 56 63 28 33.

The other day the postman whose round covers Preignac arrived at Hubert Dufour's with a curious envelope. It was addressed thus: "To the present owners of the firm Dufour-Lemoine (Château de Rouquette), thanks to the care and forwarding service of the Post Office and the officials of 33118 Sauternes". The letter came from Marcel Mugler, a citizen of Marlenheim in the *département* of the Bas-Rhin. He was returning to its homeland a label from a bottle of Château Rouquette 1933, a wine he had greatly appreciated. (I should here mention that 1933, an off-year for claret, produced excellent Sauternes thanks to a marvellous spell of weather at the end of the season.) Do you suppose the post office had any trouble in delivering this letter? Not at all! The Dufours have been in Preignac since 1760, Sadly Hubert Dufour does very little château bottling. With his old vines and the experience of his ancestors to back him up, he produces a wine full of savour.

Roy (Clos du) 🍷 → *Piada*

Saint-Amand (Château)

Commune: Preignac. **Proprietor:** Louis Ricard. Vineyard manager: Jean Gérard. Consultant oenologists: Messrs. Haimovici and Bouyx. **Size of vineyard:** 22 hectares. **Average age of vines:** 30 years. **Varieties:** 15% sauvignon, 85% sémillon. **Production:** 55,000 bottles CB. **Visits:** Tuesday to Friday from 3 to 6 p.m. Tel. 56 63 27 28. **Direct sales and by mail order:** Château Saint-Amand, Preignac, 33210 Langon. **Retail sales:** 90% of the production is sold through the Bordeaux trade.

"The origins of the estate of Saint-Amand go back to remotest antiquity, for it is said that in the fifth century AD it was the residence of Saint Amand, then Bishop of Bordeaux." I particulary like the mention of "anno Domini" which gives a certain precision to this historical note, quoted in all good faith in Féret's *Bordeaux et ses vins.* No, Saint Amand was not a contemporary of Socrates, and perhaps it seems pedantic to note that in fact the said saint was born in about the year 584 and died in 679. In other words, his life spanned the better part of the seventh century. Not knowing exactly what vocation to follow, he tried several variations: as a priest in Vendée, a preacher in Belgium, a bishop in Maestricht and, on being canonized, patron saint of brewers. And, if it is true that this great itinerant evangelist did in fact come to Bordeaux, he held no official episcopal post there. If the place called Saint-Amand is supposed to have been the summer residence of a Bordeaux bishop, we must seek another occupant – an open invitation to historical researchers. But it is true that in the Middle Ages a chapel dedicated to Saint Amand was built on this site. There are still a few vestiges of it today.

A spring is also to be found, which was reputed to have therapeutic properties. Up to the seventeenth century, tenant farmers and inhabitants of the parish of Preignac used to come daily "to take the water, to wash their linen in the cold winter weather, as the water from the said spring is warm. And every year too on the feast day of Saint-Amand, they came to wash there to cure certain illnesses, a practice of long-standing tradition." But at the end of the eighteenth century, a damper was put on this tradition by one Rousseau, a lawyer at court. He successfully increased the inheritance he had received from his father by buying adjoining plots of land and, weary of the incessant comings and goings of the drinkers of the waters (who might also have been tempted to become potential grape thieves), he decided to wall in his land, blocking at either end the road which gave access to the spring. This arbitrary denial of ancient rights was met by a tidal wave of outrage, but it seems that the lawyer won the day and consecrated his time to the fruitful production of Saint-Amand's vineyard. Curiously enough, it is one of the few *crus* mentioned by Belleyme, Louis XIV's geographer, on his famous map of the Bordeaux region.

Saint-Amand is a very good Sauternes, powerful, mellow, generally with a harmonious balance between liquorosity, acids and tannins. It smells of ripe fruit with a hint of acacia honey.

Sainte Hélène (Château de) 🍷 → *Malle*

Saint-Marc (Château)

Commune: Barsac. **Proprietor:** G.F.A. André Laulan. Director: Didier Laulan. **Size of vineyard:** 18 hectares. **Average age of vines:** 25 years. **Varieties:** 20% sauvignon, 70% sémillon, 10% muscadelle. **Production:** 40 *tonneaux*, 24,000 bottles CB. **Visits:** Didier Laulan, tel. 56 27 16 87. **Direct sales and by mail order:** in France. Château Saint-Marc, Barsac, 33720 Podensac. **Retail sales:** through Bordeaux.

André Laulan is a Barsac man from head to toe; in his soul, too, linger the shades of his ancestors: the Destracs and the Bassets who are mentioned on the parish registers of the eighteenth century. Formerly, Saint-Marc was a hunting rendezvous.

At Château Saint-Marc in about 1910: wines are being sent to Tientsin.

History relates that the Duc d'Epernon, Jean-Louis Nogaret de la Valette, and his son Bernard were very fond of the place and that they used to feast here after hunting deer or wild boar. This same first Duc d'Epernon has also left his mark in the Médoc, notably at Château Beychevelle, where according to local history boats sailing on the estuary were required to salute him by lowering their sails – *baisser la voile,* hence perhaps the name Beychevelle. In the nineteenth century the *cru* was called "Hournalas", a name which leaves no doubt as to its Gascon origins (giving an idea of heat, unless there were once bread or charcoal ovens here). Shortly before 1900, Numa Laulan found himself the sole heir of the little estate. With his natural ability as an entrepreneur, he developed simultaneously his vineyard and his clientele. His business connections extended throughout Europe into Russia and he was proud to export his production to China. Following him, his son did not display the same dynamism and it was his grandson, André Laulan, who revived the estate at the end of the Second World War. His efforts and tenacity have enabled him to get the vineyard back into perfect shape. It took him nearly ten years. Then came the deadly frosts of 1956. Everything, or practically everything, had to be started all over again. And that is what he did.

Today it is the fourth generation, represented by Didier Laulan, at the helm. His experience is hereditary but, being an oenologist as well, he also brings science to bear. This means that vinification is thoroughly controlled, followed by traditional ageing in wood. If you ask him what he thinks of his wines, he replies like a new philosopher – you would think it was Bernard-Henry Lévy talking: "Taste being an intimate perception of the individual, its result is a hedonistic sensation. This purely subjective and affective notion seems difficult to characterize according to qualitative criteria." None the less, the wines of Château Saint-Marc display a happy balance between methods ancient and modern. They are typical Barsacs: wines with stamina, vigorous with the aromas of flowers and savours of slightly spicy crystallized fruits.

Saint-Marc (Cru) ♟ → *La Tour Blanche*

Sigalas Rabaud (Château)

1er cru classé

Commune: Bommes. **Proprietor:** G.F.A. du Château Sigalas Rabaud. Director: Comte Emmanuel de Lambert des Granges. Estate manager: Jean-Louis Vimeney. Consultant oenologist: M. Hiribaren. **Size of vineyard:** 15 hectares. **Average age of vines:** 35 years. **Varieties:** 7% sauvignon, 93% sémillon. **Production:** 20,000 to 25,000 bottles CB. **Visits:** by appointment. M. Vimeney, tel. 56 63 60 62. **Direct sales and by mail order:** in France and abroad. G.F.A. du Château Sigalas Rabaud, Bommes, 33210 Langon. **Retail sales.**

The estate is a huge quadrilateral of 15 hectares with the living and working buildings at the centre. Lying on a gentle, south-facing slope, it is bounded to the south by Rayne Vigneau, to the east by Lafaurie-Peyraguey, and to the north and the

Count Emmanuel de Lambert des Granges contemplating his masterpiece.

west by Rabaud-Promis. At the time of the 1855 classification, the two Rabauds were one. As at Peyraguey, each retained its title of *Premier cru classé*. The name Rabaud belongs to a very old local family. In 1660, Marie Peyronne de Rabaud married Arnaud de Cazeau. It is known that the vineyard was already in existence in the seventeenth century and that it remained in the Cazeau family until 1819, when it was bought by Gabriel Deyme, to whom it still belonged in 1855. Henry Drouilhet de Sigalas became the new owner in 1864. His son, Gaston, sold half the vineyard to Adrien Promis in 1903, resulting in a total split between the two Rabauds. Some thirty years later the two Rabauds came together again when my grandfather, Fernand Ginestet, created a company among whose shareholders were the *heritiers* Drouilhet de Sigalas (a de Sigalas daughter had married a Lambert des Granges in 1930) and Mesdames Montrelay and de La Motte-Rouge. In 1949 the Marquis de Lambert des Granges declared his intention of buying back the land which had belonged to his family. So whereas the Lannelucs took Rabaud-Promis, Sigalas Rabaud reverted to its original family.

The wines have floral notes in a complex bouquet. They can vary considerably in style from one year to the next, from finesse to power. Count Emmanuel de Lambert des Granges and his estate manager Jean-Louis Vimeney make a happy team with a united eye to quality.

Simon (Château)   ♇ ♇ ♇ ♇ ♇

Commune: Barsac. **Proprietor:** J.-H. Dufour. **Size of vineyard:** 12 hectares. **Average age of vines:** 30 years. **Varieties:** 14% sauvignon, 84% sémillon, 2% muscadelle. **Production:** 30 *tonneaux*, 24,000 bottles CB. **Visits:** M. Dufour, tel. 56 27 15 35. **Direct sales and by mail order:** in France and abroad. Château Simon, Barsac, 33720 Podensac.

Simon is a hamlet of Barsac which lies geographically near the centre of the commune. It is also one of the oldest family names in the parish. There have always been Simons in Barsac and their origins are lost in the mists of time. As for Château Simon, it has been in the Dufour family for five generations. There have always been Dufours, too, in Barsac, and their roots are as deep as those of the Simons. Over the last few decades the little vineyard has grown and now covers some twelve immaculately cultivated hectares. Recently Jean-Hugues Dufour, the present owner, planted a small proportion of muscadelle vines. The chosen proportions of this variety (see the technical notes above) seem to me very judicious. I might even say "ideal" were I not afraid of making a hard-and-fast rule. At Simon, modern techniques and tradition cross paths and come together. The vats are modern. The collection of *barriques* is renewed gradually. The wine is generally pale in colour with a discreet balance between alcohol and sugar, yet without being unctuous. The second label of Château Simon is Château Grand Mayne, which produces lesser wines. I am not always in favour of these so-called second labels, but in this case. I have to admit that it is of considerable benefit to the principal wine of the *cru* (and to the detriment of the secondary one).

Simon Carretey (Château) ♟ → Gravas

Suau (Château)

2e cru classé

Commune: Barsac. **Proprietor:** Roger Biarnès. Consultant oenologists: Albert Bouyx and C.E.I.OE. in Cadillac. **Size of vineyard:** 6.5 hectares. **Average age of vines:** 15 to 25 years. **Varieties:** 15% sauvignon, 85% sémillon. **Production:** 18,000 bottles CB. **Visits:** weekdays. Tel. 56 27 20 27. **Direct sales and by mail order:** in France and abroad. Roger Biarnès, Château de Navarro, 33720 Illats. **Retail sales.**

To introduce this *cru*, I should like to quote from Michel Dovaz who, in his *Encyclopédie des Crus Classés du Bordelais*, retraced the stages of its history with perfect clarity: "This château is extremely old. In the eighteenth century it belonged to Henry de Carneau, lieutenant-general of the King's armies. In 1722, his daughter married the Marquis Pierre de Lur Saluces into whose hands the estate passed on the death of his father in 1745. Claude-Henri Hercule de Lur Saluces, who received it as a legacy, sold it in 1793. After the Marions and then the Chaines, the Garros family administered it for seventy years. Madame Pouchappadesse, née Garros, sold the vineyard in 1967 to Monsieur Biarnès, retaining only the château for her personal use. Monsieur Biarnès was already the proprietor of Domaine de Coy (in the commune of Sauternes) and Château Navarro in the commune of Illats (red and white Graves, Cérons). Château Suau, a *cru classé*, is vinified at Château Navarro, the Biarnès' residence."

Château Suau lies between the railway and the R.N. 113. The vineyard is in one continuous stretch, facing east. Its soil is made up of supple, soft clay, slightly sandy and easy to work. There are several plots with reddish, slightly gravelly land on a bed of limestone. I find Hubrecht Duijker over-severe in his criticism of Suau: "Barsac with a discreet but unconvincing perfume, lacking a degree of richness and depth. A wine which barely holds its place in the *crus classés*." Suau's perfume is not discreet, it is subtle. As it unfolds, it reveals its many vegetal layers: vervain and camomile, fern and linden. It does not spread out its riches, it rather lets its delicacy peek out. As for its depth, does Hubrecht Duijker hope to drown his reader in a 175 glass? Suau's flavour is gently penetrating, tender and persistent, unctuous without being obsequious, melting in the mouth but lively on the palate. It is one of those modern Barsacs whose easy style contrasts strongly with the massive classical wines. Relatively high acidity can generally be found (in the '83, for example), but it is balanced out by sweet savours reminiscent of English toffee.

In the nineteenth century, moreover, England revelled in the wines of Suau, which were imported by the barrel-load. The Biarnès do not age their wine in wood. It is subjected to cold treatment and light filtering with an earth filter of the Kieselguhr type. This is a tried and tested technique which is very successful in Burgundy. But let us not start another war between the Ancients and Moderns. I raise my glass of Suau '82 to the health of M. Biarnès and his son, to the innovating oenologists and, as my glass is already empty, I will fill it to the brim with '85 to drink a toast to all wine lovers who are in on Suau's secret.

Suduiraut (Château)

1er cru classé

Commune: Preignac. **Proprietor:** S.A.R.L. Château Suduiraut. Estate manager: M. Pascaud. **Size of vineyard:** 83 hectares. **Average age of vines:** 35 years. **Varieties:** 20% sauvignon, 80% sémillon. **Production:** 100 *tonneaux*. **Visits:** Monday to Friday. M. Pascaud, tel. 56 63 27 29. **Direct sales and by mail order:** Madame Frouin, marketing manageress, 95 rue Jouffroy, 75017 Paris. **Retail sales:** through Bordeaux.

In the time of good King Henri IV, Suduiraut was known as *"le cru du Roy"*. It was at this time that the old feudal manor was burned to the ground, doubtless as a result of the religious wars which raged over all the Langon region at the instigation of the terrible first Duc d'Epernon, the implacable and bloody Jean-Louis Nogaret de La Valette, who was in permanent conflict with the magistrates of the Bordeaux Parlement and who brooked no opposition to his imperious, almost regal authority (see the volume on Saint-Julien in this series). Before coming to the Suduiraut family, who gave it their name, the estate was owned by the Duroys, as witness their coat-of-arms with ermine, which is engraved on the pediment of the garden façade. The uniting of the two heraldic blazons proves that these families were linked together, probably in the second half of the eighteenth century. The château of today, constructed in about 1670, foreshadows the magnificent architecture of Louis XIV's reign. In my opinion, it is the most beautiful wine château in this style in the whole of the Bordeaux region. The grace of its proportions, the harmonious arrangement of the façades, the robust yet elegant working buildings: all unite to give it a majestic and triumphal appearance, full of pomp but never pompous. You almost expect to see Sacha Guitry in a Louis XIV wig strolling with the noble but arthritic gait of the Sun King. A functional beauty emerges from

Monsieur Pascaud, the cellar master.

Few châteaux in Sauternes have the discreet harmony of Suduiraut.

the whole picture, exempt from all "superfluity" as Colbert and Vauban used to say when speaking of the ornamental extravagances of certain royal decorators who were attempting to flatter Bordeaux's wealthy families. And yet there is nothing austere. This is not Port-Royal. A high pediment and hanging balcony on carved stone corbels add the most perfect touch of elegance. And the park, planned by Le Nôtre, makes a flawless green setting for this architectural jewel.

At the time of the Revolution the Suduiraut estate passed into the hands of the Castelnaus, already proprietors of the *cru* Pugneau in Preignac. A quarter of the latter went to enlarge the Suduiraut estate, which then covered some 200 hectares. The size and disposition of its land has not changed since the beginning of the nineteenth century. At the time of the 1855 classification there were 70 hectares of vines, a considerable amount at that time. Shortly before, the *cru* had been passed to a certain Guilhot (or Guillot) who accordingly became Guillot de Suduiraut, founder in his turn of a highly esteemed family in the region with several branches in the area today.

In 1873 the Guillot heirs sold the property to Henri Rabourdin who did not keep it long, selling it at a comfortable profit to the engineer Emile Petit de Forest. The area under vines was then increased to 100 hectares and from that time on has not changed greatly. One special feature is that Suduiraut was one of the first Sauternes *crus* to abandon wooden posts to support the vines, using wire instead, as had been done at Château Durfort-Vivens in Margaux. It appears that the impeccable condition of the vineyard was responsible for its suffering less than its neighbours from the ravages of phylloxera in the 1880s. The estate's worth had already been recognized and rewarded by the Great Gold Medal awarded by the ministry, a distinction much coveted at that time. Suduiraut then passed from Madame Petit de Forest to Léopold Fonquernie. Tribute should be paid to this continuing line of distinguished owners. In the eventful histories of the great Bordeaux châteaux it is 177 comparatively rare , over two centuries, for a *cru* not to become unworthy of its fame. The name of Château Suduiraut has remained constantly and consistently well deserving of its reputation. The sole *Premier cru classé* of Preignac has always been the standard-bearer of the commune, and many medals have crowned its successive and successful vintages. Today it is the Fonquernie heirs who, under the personal direction of Madame Frouin, preside over the destiny of this temple of quality. But a family trust is notoriously difficult to manage. Preliminary discussions on the subject have recently taken place and even if on this occasion the ownership of Château Suduiraut has not changed, it's not beyond the bounds of possibility that vintages to come may see a newcomer impose his rule over the *cru*.

The wines have a superb straw colour and resist oxidation well. They have aromas typical of the *Grands Crus*: honey, elder, with a concentration typical of the sémillon. Their savour is rich and deep and, even in the cold years, has an exquisite finesse and is sometimes extraordinarily long in the mouth. Yes indeed, Suduiraut's excellence is undying and I hold it in the highest esteem. Nothing could persuade me to change my mind.

Terrefort (Domaine de) ♟♟♟♟♟

Commune: Sauternes. **Proprietor:** Bernard Fage. **Size of vineyard:** 1.5 hectares. **Average age of vines:** 35 years. **Varieties:** 1% sauvignon, 79% sémillon, 20% muscadelle. **Production:** 3 *tonneaux*. **Direct sales and by mail order:** in France. Monsieur Bernard Fage, Pasquette, Sauternes, 33210 Langon.

Brother Bernard-Louis Fage is a member of the traditional congregation of the Sainte-Famille. Through his ancestors he owns Terrefort, a little estate particularly blessed by the Almighty, for its cultivation has been a religion in itself for the Lafon-Fages for more than two centuries. The previous master of the estate, Désir Lafon, was a cantor at the parish church in Sauternes. His golden voice led the congregation. The office was celebrated with wine from Terrefort. The same is still true today in many religious communities Bétharram, Trappist monks '(and others), who demand natural wine for their supernatural offices. And that is why this *cru* is impossible to find in the secular trade. I would willingly turn myself into a monk for twenty-four hours to enjoy the blessing of being able to taste it. But I wager that even the "high pontiff of wine", my friend the late Alexis Lichine himself, never lifted a glass to his epicurean lips. Truly Terrefort is a wine made in Heaven!

Trillon (Château) ♟♟♟♟♟

Commune: Sauternes. **Proprietor:** Jean-Claude Guicheney. **Size of vineyard:** 20 hectares. **Average age of vines:** 20 to 25 years. **Varieties:** 10% sauvignon, 80% sémillon, 10% muscadelle. **Production:** 50 *tonneaux*, 25,000 bottles CB. **Direct sales:** to private customers at various fairs throughout France. Jean-Claude Guicheney, Château Trillon, Sauternes, 33210 Langon. Tel. 56 63 60 21. **Retail sales:** in bulk.

Homeland becomes a homestead.

"I bought this land because I was born here." Once Jean-Claude Guicheney has said this, he has already said nearly everything about what is most important to him. His father was estate manager of the property belonging to the Dubernard-Trillons. He began in life as a farm-worker after going to agricultural college at Blanquefort. "My college friends are practically all agricultural advisers. I advise myself." In 1967, after rifling his savings account and taking advantage of a grant for young agricultural workers, he bought Trillon and established himself there. Working with determination – you might even say doggedness – he looks after everything himself: cultivation, vinification, ageing, bottling. To ensure financial liquidity, he sells part of his harvest in bulk to the trade. But the nectar destined for his private clients he bottles and labels himself. It can be found at the Salon de l'Agriculture in Paris, at the Foire in Nancy, and more. Not content with selling, he delivers the orders in person. "In that way, you are sure of being paid sooner and you can sell a drop more to the odd cousin or neighbour of your client." Jean-Claude Guicheney is frank and honest. As honest as his Trillon is delicious. "The '86? In a word, it is sumptuous. To mark the fact, I put it into new *barriques*. But I won't let it go for less than 200 francs a bottle!" That is but a drop in the ocean when you are buying pure gold. He has continued to mine the same golden seam in later vintages.

Villefranche (Château)

Commune: Barsac. **Proprietor:** Henri Guinabert. Consultant oenologist: Pierre Sudraud. **Size of vineyard:** 7 hectares. **Average age of vines:** 20 years. **Varieties:** 10% sauvignon, 85% sémillon, 5% muscadelle. **Production:** 31 *tonneaux*. **Visits:** preferably by appointment. Tel. 56 27 16 39. **Direct sales and by mail order:** in France. Monsieur Guinabert, Villefranche, Barsac, 33720 Podensac. **Retail sales:** half of the production is sold through the trade.

The Guinaberts has been in Sauternes since 1453 and have owned the estate of Villefranche since the middle of the seventeenth century. In the reign of Louis XIV the main house had a dove cote, a singular privilege at that time, indicating lordly status. The Guinaberts know Villefranche through and through for they have in their possession all the family archives since the time of Louis XVI. So they can tell you in minutest detail all about the modifications carried out on the estate over the generations. There is sufficient material here for a treatise devoted solely to the saga of The Guinaberts at Villefranche. One of these days some university or other could undertake such research.

As regards the wine, a splendid collection of old vintages proves the aptitude of the *cru* for ageing. The vineyard is on the plateau of the Haut-Barsac, near the Ciron. For Henri Guinabert, there can be no doubt: the balance of the soil is responsible for the balance of the wine. The gravel and sand ensure finesse. The limestone gives power, the clay unctuousness. The blend of grape varieties is classic. The wines of Château Villefranche are archetypes of Barsac, with delicate perfumes in which can be detected vanilla and nutmeg; great finesse, distinguished elegance, subtle softness. The '82 is sensational. The latest vintages are also very good value.

Vimeney (Château) 🍷 → Lafaurie-Peyraguey

Voigny (Château)

Commune: Preignac. **Proprietor:** G.A.E.C. Bon Frères (Jean-Aimé and Didier-Noël Bon). **Size of vineyard:** 21 hectares. **Average age of vines:** 35 years. **Varieties:** not divulged. **Production:** 58 *tonneaux*. **Direct sales:** G.A.E.C. Bon Frères, Ch. Voigny, Preignac, 33210 Langon. Tel. 56 63 28 29. **Retail sales:** in bulk.

sold in bulk

The name of Château Voigny is of recent date. It was first seen in the 1969 edition of Cocks and Féret's *Bordeaux et ses Vins*. The Bon family bought the vineyard in 1949 and the estate is consecrated to producing wines in bulk. It appears that the average age of the vines is thirty-five years. But the proportions of varieties remain a mystery – perhaps they are a state secret. Nor can you visit the cellars. Are we to believe that there is there a secret there too?

Yquem (Château d')

1er cru classé supérieur

Commune: Sauternes. **Proprietor:** Comte A. de Lur Saluces. Production manager: Francis Mayeur. Vineyard manager: Yves Laporte. Cellar master: Guy Latrille. **Size of vineyard:** 102 hectares. **Average age of vines:** 23 years. **Varieties:** 20% sauvignon, 80% sémillon. **Production:** 70,000 bottles CB. **Visits:** by appointment, strictly for professionals. Office, tel. 56 44 07 45. **Sales by mail order:** in France. Château d'Yquem, Sauternes, 33210 Langon. **Retail sales:** through Bordeaux.

He liked light-coloured shoes and pale blue pocket handkerchiefs. He was a man of artistic gestures who spoke with suave distinction occasionally tinged with a hint of affectation. He was single and his dogs held a high place in his affections. Anybody meeting him for the first time would have found it difficult to imagine that Bertrand, Marquis de Lur Saluces, came from a very old military family which with each generation, from the dawn of the fifteenth century, had successively built up a reputation as courageous military officers and skilled swordsmenship. But the good and gentle Marquis had certain phobias and caprices which made him as assertive in character as he was unusual. He claimed to be a monarchist, but was the first to stand to attention when the Marseillaise was played. He abhorred vulgarity, but used to like to tell earthy stories when among friends. He affected a certain disdain towards the great merchant families of the Chartrons, but did not scorn to sit to the right of the mistress of the house at any dinner in their houses. He used to express himself with a certain meekness, tinged with detachment, but his reasoning lent force to whatever he said and his opinions were authoritative. He had a fine intellect with wide literary and artistic knowledge which he never flaunted, except occasionally to poke gentle fun at some pedant or other. He was a man of many parts and roles which he played to perfection according to the solemnity of the occasion, the utility of the encounter or the futility of the fleeting moment. He had formed a number of long-lasting hatreds although no one was able to explain why. As an example, I recall his reply, a forceful tirade, when it was mentioned one day in front of him that P... had just set off on a voyage to India. He exclaimed (in his typically deadpan way): "Is that so? Well I hope he gets lacerated by tigers, crushed by snakes and (making the gestures suited to each action) trodden under foot by elephants!" And he meant it. You would certainly not feel at ease if you knew you were on the Marquis's blacklist.

He was one of the outstanding figures in Bordeaux from the thirties up to his death in 1968, a figure of fable and legend whose species died with him. For forty years he was president of the Union des Crus Classés of the Gironde but he also took on the presidency of the national committee for the promotion of French wines, an organization which could not have dreamt of finding a more prestigious

In the morning mist, harvesters make their way to the starting point.

ambassador: "Anacreon, Horace, Virgil, Ovid, our minstrels and our troubadours, Ronsard and the Pléiade, all our classical writers and all our romantics have sung the fame of wine. And so it has been throughout the whole of the civilized world. Nature knows no product of the earth which has enjoyed such prestige from the beginning of time, nor one which has been sung by the poets in such exultant tones, providing their inspiration with its richest themes and finest sounding notes." (Preface to *Vin de France dans l'Histoire,* 1953).

Dorling Kindersley published in 1986 a marvellous book entitled "Yquem", by Richard Olney and Michel Guillard. The first wrote the text, the second was responsible for the photographs. It is a work to be taken in sips, with delight. I recommend this splendid book to the lover of fine wine if he wishes to know more of the realities of Yquem and to feast his eyes on exquisite images. Let honour be given where honour is due. Yquem represents the archetype of vititcultural classicism and fame. It is right and proper that its pre-eminence should be illustrated in this superb manner way. In the book, Richard Olney speculates on the origins of noble rot. I have already covered this point in the first part of this book. But, like him, I give no credence to the legend which has it that late harvesting began quite by chance in 1847, when Romain-Bertrand de Lur Saluces, after a hunting-party in Russia, returned to Sauternes several weeks late to find the harvesters obediently awaiting him and the harvest itself rotting as nobly as it could. In 1855 Yquem was acclaimed *Premier Cru supérieur.* It should be mentioned that this status is unique in the classification. The four *Premiers Crus classés*, Lafite, Latour, Margaux and Haut-Brion, were not qualified as "supérieur". Yquem is the one and only example. Today, all the *crus classés*, from the first growths to the fifths, take advantage of the term *"Grand Cru classé"*, which has no particular significance in the official delimitations of the classification. But at the time, the wines of Sauternes and Barsac were of course sweet ones. And it is as such that the best *crus* were classified. Rating them in this selective way reflected a long-standing qualitative hierarchy. When Thomas Jefferson visited the Langon region in 1787, the classification of the *crus* was already in existence by virtue of their sale price. We know that the wines of Yquem cost twice as much as the other "best wines", with the exception of Filhot and Suduiraut which, in certain good years, came close to the highest price, that is around eight hundred livres the

182

The new cellar for ageing the wine.

tonneau. In the nineteenth century Yquem even exceeded the prices fetched by the red *Premiers*, sometimes doubling them.

"The tsars of Russia were loyal clients and, more recently, Joseph Stalin's admiration for Yquem was such that he begged the Marquis Bertrand de Lur Saluces to send him cuttings of the vines, so that he might extract this miraculous nectar from Russian terrain! On Yquem's office walls faded photographs crowd in upon one another, memories of visits by personalities as diverse as Josephine Baker and the Lord Mayor of London and, in its visitors books, the signatures of Alfonso XIII, King of spain, and his suite vie with those of members of the Russian Imperial Guard and of celebrities from the worlds of the arts and the sciences", (Richard Olney, *Yquem 1986).*This rapid description of Yquem's fame gives just a brief idea of its extent. For Yquem shares its fame with no one. It is unique. "I do not call Yquem a wine, for other wines exist and Yquem is unique", wrote Frédéric Dard, the French thriller writer and wine lover. I know no other example of such uniqueness in the works of man, be they in the field of art, science or, as is the case here, the produce of the land. This glory is total and complete. The *chef d'œuvre* is masterly indeed.

But this supremacy is not without its demands. Maintaining the exceptional reputation of Yquem goes hand in hand with the sovereign tradition of the Lur Saluces family. The motto of the House of Orange, "I shall maintain", could well be inscribed on every label. The new lord of Yquem, Alexandre, Comte de Lur Saluces (see the entry at the beginning of the catalogue) is a master of the art of conservatism. I dare wager that before taking the least decision, he asks himself "What would Uncle Bertrand have done?" It cannot be easy constantly to mediate between the present and the traditions of the past. Before him, the Marquis had called on another of his nephews, Baron Louis Hainguerlot, who today is a director of Moët and Chandon. The two personalities were too often in conflict for the relationship to last and Alexandre was called on to learn the family business. He adapted himself with remarkable suppleness to Yquem's complex syncretism and his uncle's idiosyncrasies. Heir to six centuries of the old nobility, of which five belonged to the Sauternes region and two particularly to the land of Yquem, Alexandre de Lur Saluces stood firm as valiant guardian of the noble house, a sort of farmer-general whose ideology of perfection is translated into maintaining excellence. So much so 183

Yquem, a vast and beautiful estate which inspires admiration.

that, as in the days of the marquis, after the concert given during the Bordeaux May music festival in the inner courtyard of the château, the guests are still served Yquem, champagne or orange juice and nothing else. So at Yquem you do not expect to see any revolutionary change, as if there were no place for bold or rash initiatives, the creation of a new vintage every year being about the only, and certainly the most prized change permitted!

"With the exception of the casks, the vinification equipment at Yquem has an antiquated charm and an aura of deeply entrenched tradition to which, one senses, Alexandre de Lur Saluces's sentimental attachment is much greater than that of Pierre Meslier (estate manager of Yquem till 1990. Editor's note). He delights in

recounting the visits of the oenological and technological avant-garde, their horror
at the venerable poverty of the equipment and, often, a downright refusal to believe that this is really what is used, or that it is physically possible for an estate
the size of Yquem to make wine only with the help of these funny little old ma-
chines." (Richard Olney, *op. cit.*) The visitor to the Bordeaux area can justifiably be
amazed by the contrast which exists today between Yquem and the *Premiers Crus
classés* red wines. The latter have made tremendous strides over the last fifteen
years with impressive capital investments, so overtly emphasizing their perpetual
quest for prestige. At Yquem, things are conceived with greater serenity and the
cult of progress does not necessarily express itself through the acquisition of the most

sophisticated machinery. At Yquem, the true religion is that of a job well done in accordance with the best tried and tested traditions. Each harvest proceeds with the same ritual and the same rites as it did more than a century ago. By its total quiescence, Yquem has determined the parameters of quintessence. There is one huge and costly concession to possible improvements: Alexandre de Lur Saluces has just completed the construction of an enormous cellar of some 2,500 square metres, capable of storing all the casks of the three years in the process of ageing. Though proud of this effort, the proprietor concludes: "This sizeable new creation does not fundamentally change life at Yquem." But he does not hide his intention of controlling temperatures better in order to limit the level of volatile acidity. In the past, Yquem was marked by certain excesses in this respect. I recall the anger of the Marquis when he was told that his 1959 was not legal. Alexandre comments: "The old Yquems considerably exceeded the levels of volatile acidity which are permitted today; but they in no way harmed the *cru*'s reputation. It is more a question of scruple as regards the law than oenological obsession." (And indeed, in the last century, did not Bertall speak of "the extravagance of perfection"?)

"One glass of wine per vine." This is the classic ratio which gives an idea of the extraordinary modesty of the yield. It can be demonstrated in the following way: there are 7,000 vines to the hectare over an extent of 100 hectares producing about 70,000 bottles every year. That is to say, ten vines to fill a bottle. All notion of profitability goes by the board on this basis. Compared with the famous great Médocs, we can say that one bottle of Yquem at 600 francs is three and a half times "cheaper" than a bottle of Lafite-Rothschild or Latour at 300 francs. For several years now, Château d'Yquem has had its own regulating stock allowing it to market, up to the present time, 66,000 bottles yearly. Recently a revision of its land register has been envisaged. A few extra hectares will be added to the vineyard by the acquisition of land nearby or already within the vineyard. Production will be progressively increased by about 10%, the yields per hectare remaining of course unchanged. But each successive year does not always produce 70,000 bottles of nectar. Every *barrique* undergoes a strict examination before the honour of the noble label may be conferred upon it. I quote from Richard Olney's book the fol-

1964	0%	1968	10%	1972	0%	1976	90%	1980	80%
1965	50%	1969	60%	1973	12%	1977	30%	1981	80%
1966	80%	1970	80%	1974	0%	1978	15%	1982	33%
1967	90%	1971	80%	1975	80%	1979	40%	1983	80%

lowing statistics covering twenty years, which show the proportion of each harvest granted the "Yquem" label. If we calculate the overall average of these percentages, it becomes clear that over the total period, Yquem presented only 50% of its production as its own wine. But the label "Y" should also be mentioned. This is the one used for wines which are vinified as dry with a "Bordeaux Blanc" appellation. This was one of the creations of the Marquis in 1959, an idea which has spread, for there are many Sauternes *crus* today which now make this type of secondary product in which the proportion of sauvignon is generally higher than in the wines of Sauternes. These dry white wines, produced by *crus classés* or *bourgeois*, are not properly speaking second labels but complementary wines, appearing particularly in years when there has been little botrytis.

By comparison with the other *Grands Crus* of the valley of the Ciron, Yquem has a distinctive personality. Over and above the way in which the wine is made, the prime reason for this difference is geological. As early as 1868 Professor Auguste Petit-Lafitte had put his finger on this fact: "Because of exceptional geological conditions in the area, Yquem's vineyard lies on a subsoil made up of clay, of varying colour but principally yellow-brown, mingled with round pebbles and sometimes

Another vision of the past: the estate workers' grocery cooperative no longer exists.

with more or less abundant particles of limestone. The gravel covering this subsoil scarcely exceeds a depth of thirty centimetres, on average over the whole estate. At Yquem, for reasons it would be difficult to explain, the beds of clay have been spared and it is on these smooth beds, which today form the elegant hill serving as the château's foundation, that a fine layer of gravel has spread out." Because of the clayey nature of the soil, drainage is essential for the healthy upkeep of the vines. Glazed earthenware drainpipes, laid a hundred years ago, ensure the healthy condition of the subsoil. Their subterranean network stretches for some hundred kilometres and great pains are taken to see that it is kept in good repair. Moreover, if it were not so maintained, the consequences would be visible at once: the vines would become suffocated by an excess of water and their leaves would turn white before the plant died.

When the former estate manager, Pierre Meslier, observed any such anomaly, he diagnosed it at once: "There must be a drain blocked or broken." At Yquem, if the vines themselves distil their precious liquor, it is mainly thanks to the work of capable agronomists, acting as plumbers of the land. Before Romain-Bertrand de Lur Saluces put this tremendous work in hand towards the end of the last century, drainage was effected by bundles of branches buried in the earth end to end. None the less, it is true that the clay at Yquem gives it its unique character. This phenomenon is much on a par with the situation in Pomerol, where Pétrus gains its distinction from the matrix of clay in the middle of neighbouring land which is simply of gravel.

The wines of Yquem are regal. There is no possible comparison with any other sweet wines. They are not rich, but opulent. They are not thick, but unctuous. They are not ample, but enormous. They are not complex, but quintessential. (And even when, by chance, they have a hint of volatile acidity, we cannot help but indulge this as mere caprice.) Since 1975, I think that with nature's help Yquem has given constant and consistent quality. I am not speaking here of the everyday quality of an honourable *cru* but the ordinary quality of Yquem *qua* Yquem.

The king? To be sure. It alone has the right to say: "I, and none other, am Wine." In short, a liquid Louis XIV. But it is on your own palate, not in any king's palace, that its glory will be revealed.

Vintage chart for the last thirty-two years
of Sauternes and Barsac

Year	Rating out of 20	Observations
1988	18-20	The very epitome of perfect botrytization. Very great, even exceptional wines, rich in flavour, distinguished, elegant and well-structured, very concentrated and already incredibly long in the mouth. Harvesting began on October 20 with seven to eight uninterrupted pickings.
1987	8-12	A promising harvest was more often than not spoiled by bad weather. Early harvesting. Some successful wines with a lot of fruit, fine and agreeable though not big.
1986	17-19	Botrytis dominates to a great extent. Exceptionally long in the mouth, full, fine, concentrated and distinguished wines.
1985	13-16	Perfect ripeness but only average botrytization. Rather sinewy wines, very aromatic with plenty of flavour and elegance. Now perfectly developed after five years.
1984	8-12	October 10, Cyclone "Hortense". Very varied wines, depending on the date of harvest. The best are supple and not very luscious, but well balanced, fruity and already agreeable.
1983	16-18	Full, rich vintage. One of the best of the decade. Ample and complete.
1982	14-17	Slightly less concentrated wines but well balanced. Several astonishing successes.
1981	13-16	Moderate degree of botrytis whose effects were successful for those who waited. Good all-round finesse.
1980	12-15	Generally poor. Some successes. Late year with no great concentration.
1979	14-17	Harmonious wines. Well structured. Great finesse. Floral, flattering wines.
1978	12-15	Very late harvesting with little botrytis. Round and rich notwithstanding. Few secondary aromas.
1977	6-10	No botrytis. Only a few – marginally successful – wines. A dull year. Small quantity.
1976	14-18	Wine of a dry year, but very good botrytis on thoroughly ripe grapes. Wines which will develop well.
1975	15-19	Ideal harvesting. Powerful wines. Rich bouquet. Much over-ripeness. Excellent vintage.
1974	4-8	Very few *crus* declared as Sauternes or Barsac. Thin and barely sweet.
1973	10-14	Relatively good harvest. Rather nondescript wines lacking consistency.
1972	10-13	Very late harvesting. Poorly structured wines of little character.
1971	13-17	Well botrytized wines, rather rich and fruity with a good future. Can be laid down.
1970	15-18	Fine, fruity and lively wines. Rather unctuous. All-round success by and large.
1969	6-10	Cold year. Insufficient maturity and little concentration. Excessive acidity.
1968		No Sauternes-Barsac.
1967	15-19	A great success. Plenty of character. Rich ample wines. A phenomenal year.
1966	9-13	Agreeable but light wines.
1965		Hardly any Sauternes-Barsac.
1964	11-14	Very slender harvest. A few Sauternes from early harvesters.
1963		No Sauternes-Barsac.
1962	14-17	Abundant harvest giving balanced wines with plenty of character. Supple and fruity.
1961	15-19	Early harvest. Small in volume. Highly concentrated wines. Much over-ripeness. Can continue to age.
1960		Very little Sauternes-Barsac.
1959	15-19	A small but very successful harvest. Plenty of body. Floral and fruity. Generous.
1958	8-13	Well-balanced wines but lacking in concentration.
1957	10-14	Slim harvest after the 1956 frosts. Satisfactory quality generally.

In view of the wide variation in success between one cru *and another, the rating of each vintage has been bracketed to indicate the possible range of quality.*

Index of proprietors

191

Picture acknowledgements:
All the photographs in this book are by
Luc Joubert, Bordeaux
with the exception of those by Bernard Pucheu-Planté,
oenological centre, Bordeaux II University (cover, 26, 27, 28, 38, 39, 82),
Michel Guillard-Scope, Paris (17, 59, 74 bottom, 83, 182, 184, 187, 188)
and Twin, Bordeaux (129)